AS History
UNIT 2

Edexcel

Civil Rights in the USA, 1945–68

Robin Bunce and Laura Gallagher

Series Editor: Derrick Murphy

Philip Allan Updates
Market Place
Deddington
Oxfordshire
OX15 0SE

Orders

Bookpoint Ltd, 130 Milton Park, Abingdon, Oxfordshire, OX14 4SB
tel: 01235 827720
fax: 01235 400454
e-mail: uk.orders@bookpoint.co.uk
Lines are open 9.00 a.m.–5.00 p.m., Monday to Saturday, with a 24-hour message answering service. You can also order through the Philip Allan Updates website: www.philipallan.co.uk

© Philip Allan Updates 2006

ISBN-13: 978-1-84489-565-6
ISBN-10: 1-84489-565-3

This guide has been written specifically to support students preparing for the Edexcel AS History Unit 2 examination. The content has been neither approved nor endorsed by Edexcel and remains the sole responsibility of the authors.

Printed by MPG Books, Bodmin

Environmental information
The paper on which this title is printed is sourced from managed, sustainable forests.

Contents

Introduction

■ ■ ■

Content Guidance

■ ■ ■

Questions and Answers

Introduction

Aims of the unit

Unit 2: Civil Rights in the USA, 1945–68 is worth 15% of the A2 course or 30% of the AS. The unit requires knowledge of the topic and the ability to identify key features and causation. There are no sources on this exam paper, so source skills are unnecessary.

There are 60 marks available for Unit 2. In the first question up to 20 marks can be awarded for the discussion of key features, and in the second the remaining 40 marks are awarded for explanation of causation. These two skills are described below.

- **Discussion of key features** — describing selected elements of a historical process or situation in order to establish the context in which events and actions took place.
- **Explanation of causation** — analysing factors that led to a historical event or process.

Both questions for this unit require you to give clear information that answers them directly. Examiners also look for detailed and precise supporting evidence and examples to demonstrate that your statements are accurate. These examples need to be linked clearly to your argument.

It is difficult to address every issue relevant to the question in 55 minutes. Examiners therefore award full marks for answers that deal adequately, and in detail, with most of the central issues.

How to use this guide

You should use this **Introduction** to make sure you understand the layout of the exam paper, the mark scheme and the types of question asked.

The **Content Guidance** section outlines what you need to know. As you read it you should try to:

- master the vocabulary and concepts given
- establish clearly the important individuals and events which shaped the years 1945–68
- assess how much had been achieved by and for black Americans by 1968

The **Question and Answer** section of this guide provides five examples of the types of question that you will be asked. It is important to work through these, studying the A- and C-grade sample answers provided and the examiner comments. The A-grade responses, while not perfect, will give you a good idea of what is required. The C-grade responses illustrate some of the common errors made by students.

The examination paper

There are two options on Paper 6522G, Social and Political Change in Post-War Powers: The USA and China 1945–76. These are:

- Option I: Pursuing 'Life and Liberty': Civil Rights in the USA, 1945–68
- Option II: China under Mao, 1949–76

You may have studied both Options I and II, but in the exam you are required to answer questions on only one of them. For each option there are two, two-part questions. You must answer either the first or second question for the option you have chosen. You must answer both parts of the question you choose.

In a typical examination paper, the Option I questions would be in the following format:

6522G — Paper 2G

Social and Political Change in Post-War Powers: The USA and China, 1945–76

Choose EITHER Option I OR Option II for which you have been prepared and answer ONE question from your chosen option. Answer parts (a) and (b) of the question you choose.

Option I — Pursuing 'Life and Liberty': Civil Rights in the USA, 1945–68

25.   (a) Describe...   (20 marks)
       (b) Why...   (40 marks)

(Total for Question 25: 60 marks)

26.   (a) In what ways...   (20 marks)
       (b) Why, in the period...   (40 marks)

(Total for Question 26: 60 marks)

Examinable skills

Success in Unit 2 requires four fundamental skills:

- focus on the question
- selection of information
- development: elaboration and support
- integration of different factors

Focus on the question

Read the question carefully to ensure that you have noted the topic, the period and the specific issue being addressed. Look at the question below.

Why did the Black Power movement emerge in the late 1960s?

In this question, the topic is *the Black Power movement*, the period is the *late 1960s* and the specific issue is *explaining why it emerged*.

Selection of information

Once you have established what the question requires, you must decide which aspects of your own knowledge are relevant. For part (a) you will need to decide on three or four relevant factors that answer the question directly. For part (b) you will need five or six relevant factors. You must arrange these factors in a logical order to create a plan for your answer.

Development: elaboration and support

Once your structure is in place you must develop it using specific examples. Try to ensure that these are detailed. You should include:

- relevant dates
- names of people, places, institutions and events
- statistics and appropriate technical vocabulary

This information must be linked explicitly to the question, i.e. you must show how these details relate to or illustrate the point that you are making.

Integration of different factors

In order to achieve the highest marks, you must highlight links between the factors that you have selected. This could mean demonstrating the relative importance of the different factors or showing how the factors are dependent on each other.

The questions

Part (a): 20 marks

Part (a) asks you to describe a particular process, event or situation. The examiners are looking for a tightly structured answer that draws out the stages making up a specific process, or the different aspects of a particular situation. You should try to demonstrate your ability to group and order information appropriately.

A common mistake is to see this as an opportunity to 'tell the story' or to write everything you know about the topic. Answers that fall into this trap will fail to meet the requirements of the question.

You should spend about 20 minutes on this question, and your answer should cover approximately one side of the examination booklet. Although you will not have time to write a full introduction and conclusion, you should write an introductory sentence and some concluding remarks to frame your answer.

Part (b): 40 marks

The focus of this question is explaining the cause of an event or historical process. Examiners will reward accurate, precise and well-supported arguments and they look for an answer that covers a wide range of factors and indicates depth of knowledge.

Again, telling the story of how an event came about will not score well. It is expected that your answer will be arranged thematically, addressing different causes in turn; a better answer will also draw out the links between different causes.

Part (b) requires a more substantial piece of writing than part (a) because there are more marks available. It should take you about 35 minutes to write your answer, and you should aim to cover approximately two and a half sides of the examination booklet. You are expected to produce a full introduction and conclusion, which answer the question by drawing together the different threads of your argument.

Content Guidance

The **Civil Rights in the USA, 1945–68** option focuses on the struggle of black Americans for equal rights between the end of the Second World War and the death of Martin Luther King in 1968.

The specification covers four fundamental topics:
- the social and economic position of black citizens in the USA in the 1940s and 1950s, and the nature and extent of discrimination and segregation
- Martin Luther King and peaceful protest
- Black Power and the use of violence
- the extent to which civil rights had been achieved by 1968

You must be aware of the economic and social position of African-Americans in different parts of the USA in the period immediately following the Second World War, and how this position altered as the period progressed. You need to know how attitudes to civil rights changed during the period, specifically on the part of groups such as black and white Americans, and the federal and state governments. You should also understand the civil rights movement from its period of peaceful protest to the later, more militant, campaigns of the Black Power movement. Finally, you need to be able to assess the significance of the Civil Rights Act (1964) and the Voting Rights Act (1965), and the extent to which civil rights had been achieved by 1968.

This section of the guide is divided into six subsections. The first subsection gives a brief chronological overview of the period. The remaining five subsections give more detailed analysis and examine the major themes of the specification. Where appropriate, each subsection is followed by listings of concepts and key terms. Words that appear in these in these listings are emboldened in the text.

Introductory overview

The position of black Americans in 1945

The Civil War (1861–65) divided the USA into the northern states, which from 1863 fought for the nationwide abolition of slavery, and the southern states, where slavery was crucial to the economy. In spite of the northern states' victory, which resulted in the national abolition of slavery and the **emancipation** of black people, racial prejudice continued. This was especially severe in the southern states, where '**Jim Crow**' laws, enacted between 1887 and 1891, segregated housing, schooling, transport and public amenities along racial lines.

In 1896, the principle of the 'Jim Crow' laws was challenged. In *Plessy* v *Ferguson* (1896), Homer Plessy claimed that these laws were unconstitutional because they contravened the **14th Amendment**, which guaranteed the citizenship of all Americans, regardless of race. Nonetheless, the **Supreme Court** upheld the 'Jim Crow' laws and the case established the legality of 'separate but equal' treatment. It was therefore constitutional to provide different services for black and white people, as long as these services were deemed 'equal'. In practice, however, services were never equal, and in some cases state governments spent as much as ten times more on services for white people than for black people.

There were black people who were willing to fight the status quo. In the late nineteenth and early twentieth centuries, campaigners such as Booker T. Washington, W. E. B. Dubois and Marcus Garvey gave voice, in different ways, to black discontent. Dubois — sometimes described as the creator of the first Civil Rights movement — founded the National Association for the Advancement of Colored People (NAACP), which sought to overturn segregation through the courts. Garvey advocated the idea that African-Americans should leave the USA and go 'back to Africa'. Booker T. Washington, on the other hand, believed that black people should not engage in political struggle. He thought that they should seek the respect of white people through hard work.

However, most black people were not engaged in political struggle, which in any case was dangerous, with violently racist groups such as the **Ku Klux Klan** (KKK) enjoying increased support in the 1920s. Black people in the southern states had little legal protection from the KKK, and it was commonplace for African-Americans who were perceived to have challenged white dominance to be lynched.

In the northern states there was little formal segregation and only pockets of KKK activity. Nonetheless, black people were frequently denied access to well-paid jobs and adequate housing. As a result, black and white communities often developed separately.

The Second World War and the Cold War

In many ways, the Second World War was a catalyst in the development of the Civil Rights movement. First, black GIs had fought for their country and therefore considered themselves US citizens in the fullest sense. Second, GIs stationed in Britain and France observed and experienced a greater degree of racial integration than they were used to in the USA. Third, both soldiers and political leaders were struck by the contradiction of fighting Nazi racism overseas, while segregation remained an accepted and legally entrenched practice both at home and in the armed forces.

The Second World War also affected non-combatants. The war effort encouraged southern black workers to migrate north to fill jobs vacated by white people serving as soldiers. Black citizens were affected by the move north in two ways — they experienced a society with less formal segregation and they received higher wages in northern factories than they had done in southern agricultural jobs.

All of these factors led to the establishment of the Congress for Racial Equality (CORE), which was founded in 1942 to campaign for increased civil rights. CORE pioneered the strategy of non-violent direct action, organising **sit-ins** at segregated restaurants and demanding desegregation on interstate transport, with limited success.

Pressure for change increased during the early years of the **Cold War**. The USA wanted to be seen as fighting for freedom and justice against communist oppression. However, the continued racial inequalities that characterised American culture compromised the USA's ability to be the international standard bearer for liberty. These considerations led President Truman (1945–53) to commission a report entitled *To Secure These Rights* (1947), which recommended an end to segregation, anti-lynching legislation and the foundation of a Commission on Civil Rights. Furthermore, as commander in chief of the armed forces, Truman issued Executive Order 9981, in 1948, to end segregation in the armed services.

Legal and peaceful protest: 1945–64

Between 1945 and 1964 the Civil Rights movement in the southern states focused on overturning segregation in education and transport, addressing social and economic inequalities and securing political rights.

Education

In *Sweatt* v *Painter* (1950), the NAACP spearheaded action that led the Supreme Court to virtually overturn *Plessy* v *Ferguson*. However, while the Supreme Court ruled that black people must have the opportunity to receive the same level of graduate education as white people, businesses, local politicians and the public obstructed change. This demonstrated that legal victories did not necessarily produce a change in the deeply entrenched racist attitudes that characterised much of US society.

The NAACP took further action in 1954 with the landmark *Brown* v *Board of Education* case. Oliver Brown argued that public education did not provide the same level of service for black and white citizens. Specifically, he claimed that it was inequitable for his daughter to be excluded from a whites-only school five blocks from his house, and for her to be forced to attend an all-black school 20 blocks away. As a result of the Brown case, the Supreme Court explicitly outlawed racial segregation in public education facilities for two reasons. First, the doctrine of 'separate but equal' (established in *Plessy* v *Ferguson*, 1896) could never truly provide an equal public education for black and white Americans. Second, the Supreme Court recognised that *Plessy* v *Ferguson* contravened the 14th Amendment.

However, the Supreme Court stopped short of drawing up a timetable for the deseg-regation of education. Consequently, even though segregation was made illegal it continued, with the vast majority of southern politicians pledging their support for continued segregation. Even when the Brown II case of 1955 resulted in the ruling that desegregation in education should occur 'with all deliberate speed', the court failed to specify exactly when this desegregation should take place.

In 1957, the 'Little Rock Nine' (nine African-American students) set out to test educational integration by attempting to enrol at Little Rock Central High School, Arkansas. A crisis erupted when Governor Orville Faubus ordered the **National Guard** to surround the school and prevent the students from entering. President Eisenhower (1953–61) responded by sending in federal troops to enforce desegregation. Nonetheless, Governor Faubus was not prepared to admit defeat, and closed the school rather than accept integration.

Challenges to segregation in education were extended to universities in the early 1960s. In 1961, violent protests greeted James Meredith's attempts to enrol at the University of Mississippi. Robert Kennedy, the attorney general, supported Meredith's enrolment. At the same time, the state governor Ross Barnett protested publicly against the proposed desegregation. Following Meredith's admission to the university, the campus was desegregated.

By 1968, despite the cases of Brown, Little Rock and Meredith, only 42% of black American students attended desegregated schools.

Transport

'Jim Crow' laws segregated public transport as well as public schools. In 1955–56 there were two parallel attempts to desegregate public transport. Rosa Parks (a long-standing member of the NAACP) was legally obliged to move when a white passenger required her seat on a bus. Her refusal to do so led to her arrest and prosecution, and sparked the Montgomery Bus Boycott. This was an attempt by black Americans to force the desegregation of public transport, and lasted for over a year. At the same time, the NAACP mounted a legal challenge (*Browder* v *Gayle*, 1956) to the city of Montgomery and the state of Alabama transport segregation laws.

The boycott was significant for a number of reasons. First, it provided a platform for the emerging leader of the US Civil Rights movement, Dr Martin Luther King. Second, it led to the creation of another important civil rights organisation, the Southern Christian Leadership Conference (SCLC), in 1957. Third, the scale of the protest was effective in gaining widespread media attention. But it was the legal challenge, and not the boycott, that ended segregation on the buses in 1956.

The NAACP sought the national desegregation of buses and bus terminals. The Supreme Court case *Morgan* v *Virginia* (1946) had ruled that segregation on interstate travel was unconstitutional. A second case, *Boynton* v *Virginia* (1960), established that segregation in public transport terminal facilities was also illegal. CORE and the newly formed Student Nonviolent Coordinating Committee (SNCC) put this ruling to the test almost immediately, organising the Freedom Rides of 1961. CORE's mixed-race team attempted to travel from Washington DC to New Orleans on interstate buses. In both Anniston and Birmingham, the SNCC team members were victims of racist attacks. The local police were notably indifferent to these assaults. The Freedom Rides were significant as they provided a context for cooperation between the chief civil rights organisations — CORE, SNCC and the SCLC. Additionally, they focused media attention on the continuing activity of racist groups such as the KKK.

Finally, President Kennedy (1961–63) was forced to address the issues. Federal injunctions were brought out against the KKK, and Attorney General Robert Kennedy ordered the desegregation of all interstate travel. On the other hand, federal government's sympathy for the Civil Rights movement was qualified. It continued to support the incarceration of civil rights protesters as long as white attackers were dealt with in the same way.

Social and economic inequalities

Segregation was a fact of life that extended beyond education and transport. In the southern states, restaurants, libraries, parks and other local amenities were segregated routinely. By 1960 this segregation was no longer lawful, but it continued because of the obstinacy of southern white Americans. Moreover, discrimination was practised widely within employment. The early 1960s saw a series of campaigns aimed largely at challenging this social and economic segregation.

The Greensboro, North Carolina sit-ins of 1960, organised by SNCC, were non-violent protests against the unlawful segregation of a local Woolworth's canteen. Protesters were refused service but no attempt was made to evict them. This sit-in sparked a series of similar sit-ins, swim-ins, read-ins and economic boycotts, which in 2 months spread to 54 cities in nine states, with 50,000 people actively involved. By the end of 1961, over 800 towns and cities had desegregated public areas. Furthermore, Greensboro caused the creation of SNCC.

A further step was taken in 1961 when President Kennedy issued Executive Order 10925. This established the President's Committee on Equal Employment Opportunity and legally ended discrimination in all appointments by the federal government, its contractors and subcontractors. The Executive Order also gave the government the power to prosecute offenders and issue a 'Certificate of Merit' to any organisation that was shown to be an equal opportunities employer.

Following Greensboro, non-violent methods were applied in Albany, Georgia (1961–62) and Birmingham, Alabama (1963) in an attempt to overturn racial discrimination. In both cases, non-violent protests were designed to provoke racist violence, and thereby focus media attention on the ongoing struggle for equal treatment. In Birmingham, this strategy proved highly successful. Local police chief Eugene 'Bull' Connor used water cannons, dogs and strong-armed policing against unarmed protesters. To avoid the economic disruption of more boycotts, Birmingham stores began to desegregate and businesses pledged to end discriminatory employment practices. Additionally, media portrayal of the protests and Connor's response attracted increased support for the protesters from those outside the southern states. By contrast, the Albany campaign of a year earlier was not a success. Police chief Laurie Pritchett ensured that the police treated the protesters with respect. He also agreed to discussions about the end of segregation in the city. This defused the situation without leading to any concrete gains for Albany's black citizens.

The March on Washington in August 1963 was staged to draw attention to issues of segregation and black economic conditions. A quarter of a million protesters descended on Washington, DC to hear Martin Luther King's famous 'I Have a Dream' speech. The march was significant as it marked a moment of unity between the different strands of the Civil Rights movement and the Kennedy administration. Moreover, it was one of the factors that led to the passing of the Civil Rights Act of 1964 under the presidency of Lyndon B. Johnson (1963–69). Essentially, the act banned segregation and gave the government powers to enforce this ban. It also created a Fair Employment Practices Commission to address discrimination in the workplace. Economic discrimination was explicitly outlawed in any projects supported by the federal government.

Political rights

The political rights of black Americans were an essential part of the civil rights agenda. Southern states traditionally used a variety of tactics, such as **grandfather clauses** and **literacy tests**, to exclude black people from voting. In *Smith* v *Allwright* (1944), the NAACP mounted a legal challenge to black exclusion from Democratic **primary elections** in Texas. The NAACP argued that as the Democratic Party's hold on Texas was so strong, the primary election effectively selected the winning candidate. Consequently, the NAACP established successfully in this case that all-white primaries broke the provisions of the **15th Amendment**.

In 1965, King and the SCLC challenged the political exclusion of black Americans in Selma, Alabama — a city where only 335 of over 15,000 African-Americans were registered to vote. This was an important test of the influence of the Civil Rights Act in the southern states. The Selma authorities, headed by Sheriff Jim Clark, obstructed the registration of black voters with a series of irrelevant qualifying questions such as 'how many bubbles are there in a bar of soap?' Additionally, the Selma police used electric cattle prods to disperse black citizens who were queuing to vote. This ill-treatment, coupled with a series of marches from Selma to Montgomery, drew media attention to the continuing disenfranchisement of southern African-Americans. President Johnson responded by passing the Voting Rights Act (1965). This act outlawed any tests that excluded eligible US citizens from voting, such as literacy tests or tests assessing educational qualifications and moral character.

Increasing radicalisation: 1965–68

The Civil Rights Acts (1964 and 1968) and the Voting Rights Act (1965) did not mark the end of King's vision, but they did lead to a change in direction for the movement. As the Moynihan Report (commissioned by the government in 1965) revealed, black Americans throughout the USA still faced considerable social and economic hardships. For this reason, King turned his attention to issues of poverty, and moved his focus to the northern states where problems of **ghettoisation** were especially severe. In addition, King and the SCLC were concerned that their leadership and non-violent methods were not widely accepted outside the southern states.

Poor housing conditions, increased racial disturbances, and a lack of racial integration led King to choose the northern city of Chicago, Illinois as the focus for his 1966 campaign. King's strategy for dealing with ghettoisation in the north was essentially the same as his strategy for dealing with formal segregation in the south. However, as in Albany, Mayor Richard Daley refused to play into his hands, instead making ambiguous promises to improve housing conditions and implicitly rejecting King's involvement. Additionally, King was unfamiliar with northern conditions and did not enjoy the same respect from, and rapport with, northern African-Americans.

In spite of this setback in Chicago, King's final campaign was more ambitious still. The Poor People's Campaign was intended to unite poor people of all races in an attempt to 'confront the power structure' (King). He believed that a broader coalition was necessary to confront poverty because economic advancement for black Americans could take place only at the expense of the rich, the most powerful people in the USA. In this sense, the battle against poverty was much more difficult than the battle against segregation, and therefore needed a greater degree of popular support.

However, the Poor People's Campaign failed to catch the public imagination and King's support base dwindled at the same time. By 1967, the black Civil Rights movement was split clearly between those still committed to non-violence and more radical groups who believed that militant methods were necessary to fight white oppression. Furthermore, many white liberals believed that the victories of 1964 and 1965 were sufficient to guarantee black freedom and equality, and that there was no need for a continuing Civil Rights movement. Additionally, the Vietnam War monopolised the attention of radicals to the detriment of King's new campaign. The proposed march on

Washington by the Poor People's Campaign was consequently postponed to the summer of 1968, by which time King had been assassinated.

Disillusionment with King's methods was evident in the Watts Riots in Los Angeles in 1965. The black community of Los Angeles had the legal rights to use the same amenities and live in the same areas as white citizens. However, because of widespread black poverty, these rights remained largely theoretical. Many felt that King's victories had done little to improve their living conditions. Resentment at these conditions turned into violence following the arrest and brutal treatment of Marquette Frye for alleged drink-driving. Over 6 days, rioters caused $40 million worth of destruction, 14,000 troops were required to restore order, 4,000 people were arrested and 34 people were killed.

By the mid-1960s, there were a number of alternatives within the Civil Rights movement to the non-violent methods pioneered in the southern states. 'Black Power' was a slogan coined by Stokely Carmichael, a prominent member of the SNCC. The SNCC became disillusioned with Martin Luther King and his methods, and argued that white people would dominate black people as long as they remained a minority within the USA. Consequently, the SNCC adopted the principle of **self-determination** and expelled all white members from its ranks in 1966. For the 'New Afrikans' of the SNCC, self-determination meant that black Americans should establish an independent nation within the territory of the USA, of which they would form the majority.

Malcolm X, a leading spokesman for the **Nation of Islam**, came to similar conclusions, and advocated Black Pride. By this he meant that black people would gain freedom only by their own efforts. King's dream of racial integration was Malcolm X's nightmare, because he believed that integration would simply lead to the corruption of black people by white people. Malcolm X believed that black freedom could be achieved only in an all-black community, and he accused white liberals of being hypocrites. However, Malcolm X was unclear about whether this community would be a separate nation within the USA, or whether a return to Africa was necessary. Malcolm X broke with the Nation of Islam in 1964, leading to his assassination by some of its members in 1965.

The Black Panthers were another example of the militancy that characterised black politics in the late 1960s. The Black Panther Party (BPP) was founded by Huey Newton, Bobby Seale and Richard Aoki in 1966. The BPP organised an armed self-defence force that 'defended' black communities against the 'foreign occupying force' of racist white police. The BPP also had a political platform in the form of the 'Ten-Point Program', which called, among other things, for social and economic equality for black people, the exemption of black citizens from military service, freedom for all black prisoners and an end to racist policing. The program could be summed up by its first point: 'We want freedom. We want power to determine the destiny of our black community.'

The Black Power movement (a term that describes the Black Panthers and the followers of Malcolm X, as well as the CORE and SNCC after 1964) believed that the non-violent Civil Rights movement of the 1950s and early 1960s had failed to address the real issues affecting black people. Moreover, the movement believed that the strategy of working with white people for formal legal changes would never achieve black emancipation. Malcolm X's call to fight white oppression 'by all means necessary' characterised the militant methodology of Black Power. However, it would be incorrect to view Black Power as a coherent movement with shared aims and ideals. Rather, the phrase is used as a blanket term to describe disparate groups that shared the belief that the black community should reject the goal of racial integration and the methods of non-violence in favour of Black Nationalism.

Glossary

14th Amendment — an addition made to the US Constitution in **1868** stating that anybody born in the USA has the full rights of citizenship and 'equal protection of the law'. No state government can take these rights away.

15th Amendment — an addition made to the US Constitution in **1870** stating that all citizens have the right to vote regardless of their race.

Cold War — an ideological conflict between the capitalist USA and the communist USSR following the end of the Second World War. The Cold War was characterised by international tension between capitalist and communist countries, which occasionally turned into military conflict, for example in the Vietnam War.

emancipation — the act of liberation.

ghettoisation — the isolation of black people in a specific geographical area, often with poor facilities.

grandfather clause — following the 15th Amendment, some southern states introduced laws, which were not based on race, to exclude black people from voting. The grandfather clause excluded people whose grandfathers had not been enfranchised.

'Jim Crow' — a slang term used to describe laws created in some southern states to enforce racial segregation.

Ku Klux Klan — a white supremacist organisation, founded in 1865, and dedicated to overturning the rights won by black people following the American Civil War. The group was most influential in the southern states.

literacy tests — following the 15th Amendment, some southern states introduced laws, which were not based on race, to exclude black people from voting. Literacy tests excluded all those who were unable to read and write. However, in practice the law was applied only to black citizens and illiterate whites were therefore permitted the vote.

National Guard — a military force designed for home defence. It is a national organisation but is organised along state lines, so under normal circumstances it is available for the state governor to call upon in times of emergency. However, it remains under the ultimate control of the president, who acts as commander in chief of all the armed forces.

Nation of Islam — a religious and political organisation founded by Wallace Fard Muhammad in 1930. The organisation preaches a form of Islam that claims all people were originally black until the artificial creation of white people by an evil scientist. White people are therefore considered to be inferior to black people. Black people are encouraged to have nothing to do with whites and to work hard and live moral lives.

primary elections — elections held by the Democrats and Republicans in which voters select the candidates from each party to be entered for subsequent elections.

self-determination — the belief that people should be free to govern themselves.

sit-ins — a form of non-violent protest in which activists refuse to leave an area until their demands are met.

Supreme Court — the highest court of appeal in the USA. The Supreme Court has the right to strike down any laws that it believes to be unconstitutional.

The NAACP and the Supreme Court

What is the NAACP?

The National Association for the Advancement of Colored People (NAACP) was founded by a multiracial group of campaigners in 1909. It was originally called the National Negro Committee, and its founders included Ida Wells-Barnett, W. E. B Dubois and William English. The NAACP was established to ensure that the rights (in the broadest sense) of all people were upheld, and to fight racial hatred and discrimination. In its early years, the NAACP publicly opposed the establishment of segregation in federal government offices, which was introduced by President Woodrow Wilson. It also put pressure on the government to reject the appointment of Supreme Court justices who were in favour of segregation or who were ambivalent towards lynching.

Between 1945 and 1960, the NAACP used legal methods to challenge segregation in the southern states. Typically, it provided legal support for black citizens involved in court cases opposing segregation. The most prominent of the NAACP's legal team was Special Counsel Thurgood Marshall, who became the first African-American Supreme Court Justice in 1967. From the late 1950s, members of the NAACP became involved in and organised non-violent direct action — these actions were often sanctioned by the NAACP leadership. For example, Rosa Parks and the leaders of the Greensboro sit-ins were all members of the NAACP.

Why did the NAACP focus on education?

The Brown case and Brown II (1954–55) were two high-profile examples of the NAACP in action. The NAACP focused on education because this was an area in which it could be demonstrated clearly that black and white citizens were not being treated as equals. For example, it was possible to compare class sizes, resource levels, teachers' salaries and state funding. It was shown that classes in white schools, for instance, were smaller by a third than in black schools, and in South Carolina in 1949 an average of $179 was spent on the education of each white child but only $43 was spent on each black student.

The NAACP also focused on education because it believed that changing the educational opportunities of black students was the first step towards improving their employment opportunities and therefore their social and economic status. Moreover, educated black citizens would be better equipped to fight for their civil rights. Finally, the treatment of children was an emotive issue, so the NAACP was likely to have public backing when challenging inequalities in education.

Use of legal methods by the NAACP

The NAACP used legal methods because its members recognised that segregation had legal foundations (in the case of *Plessy* v *Ferguson*) and that segregation could not be overturned until the law was changed. The NAACP's strategy was to argue that 'Jim Crow' laws were unconstitutional. Its members appealed to the 14th and 15th Amendments to the US Constitution, which grant citizenship to all people born or naturalised in the USA, and asserted that the right to vote could not be denied on the grounds of race.

In the decade following the Second World War, the Supreme Court was the most active branch of government in advancing civil rights. The Supreme Court is the USA's highest court of law. The nine Supreme Court Justices have final authority to interpret the Constitution, and they have the power to rule that laws made by the US Congress and state legislatures are unconstitutional. The NAACP's goal was to persuade the Supreme Court that 'Jim Crow' was unconstitutional and therefore to order the institutions of segregation to be dismantled.

The NAACP's approach represented a belief that it was possible to work within the US system for the advancement of civil rights. It also indicated the belief that a ***de jure*** end to 'Jim Crow' was a necessary precondition for racial equality. The NAACP was not unconcerned with informal, or ***de facto***, changes, but its members believed that permanent change could come about only through legal changes made by overturning *Plessy* v *Ferguson*.

NAACP successes, 1944–60

Between 1944 and 1960, the NAACP fought a number of high-profile court cases, challenging segregation in the areas of education, transport and suffrage. While these court cases were invariably successful in achieving *de jure* change, *de facto* change was often slow to follow.

In the first decade after the Second World War, the NAACP focused primarily on education. In the cases of *Sweatt* v *Painter* (1950), *Brown* v *Board of Education, Topeka* (1954) and *Brown II* (1955), the Supreme Court acknowledged that the standard of separate education provision for black American students was significantly lower than that enjoyed by white students. The results of both *Sweatt* v *Painter* and *Brown* v *Board of Education* therefore affirmed the right of students to participate in racially integrated education. However, these *de jure* victories did not lead to immediate *de facto* changes. For example, while *Sweatt* v *Painter* outlawed segregation in higher education institutions, black students were still routinely excluded from universities — as the 1962 case of James Meredith illustrates. Similarly, the Brown II ruling, that desegregation of schools should take place 'with all deliberate speed', was necessary only because the initial Brown ruling did not precipitate any significant change. Brown II failed to set a clear timetable for desegregation, and therefore even after this legal victory 97% of black students remained in segregated schools.

Transport was another area in which there was much NAACP activity. In *Morgan* v *Virginia* (1946) and *Boynton* v *Virginia* (1960) the NAACP exploited the ambiguity of segregation on interstate transport. In theory, a black passenger could board a desegregated bus in the northern states, but on entering the southern states the passenger would immediately be subject to the laws of segregation. *Morgan* v *Virginia* established that interstate transport could not be segregated legally — but this was only a partial victory, as bus companies were able to capitalise on the loophole where the court case did not apply to bus terminals. As a result, *Boynton* v *Virginia* was necessary to revoke segregation across the whole interstate network. Once again, though, the *de jure* victory of 1960 did not lead to an immediate *de facto* change, as the Freedom Rides of 1961 demonstrated.

Desegregation of the Montgomery buses was altogether more successful, owing to the combination of the NAACP's legal challenge and the SCLC's boycott. *Browder* v *Gayle* (1956) led to a *de jure* victory and was followed up immediately by *de facto* desegregation of Montgomery's bus services as a result of the year-long boycott.

The NAACP's achievement from 1945 to 1960 is contradictory. The main thrust of its campaign was to overturn the 'Jim Crow' laws legally. While it succeeded in doing this, this achievement on its own did not end *de facto* segregation in the southern states. The NAACP was more successful in inspiring young activists who chose a different strategy from its own, allying themselves with the non-violent, civil disobedience campaigns of the SCLC, SNCC and CORE. It was the activities of grass-roots members of the NAACP in the Greensboro sit-ins, the Montgomery Bus Boycott and the Freedom Rides that arguably did more to end *de facto* segregation than the high-profile court cases at the centre of the NAACP's official strategy.

Glossary

de facto — actual and real, backed up by actions. For example, *de facto* segregation occurs when African-Americans and white people live in separate housing areas and attend different schools in spite of formal legal equality.

de jure — backed by law, either state or federal.

Martin Luther King

Background and ideology

Martin Luther King was born in Atlanta, Georgia in 1929 and enjoyed a relatively privileged upbringing. He graduated from Morehouse College with a degree in sociology in 1948 and attended Crozier Theological Seminary before entering the University of Boston, where in 1955 he received his PhD in theology. Prior to his involvement in the Civil Rights movement he was, like his father, a Baptist minister.

King's education and religious beliefs informed his approach to the civil rights struggle and his aspirations for his fellow black citizens. Christianity inspired King's aims and his methods — he believed that the campaign for civil rights was God's will, as God had created all humanity in his own image. Jesus's message of compassion and non-retaliation characterised King's non-violent approach towards protest and his political opponents.

King believed that civil rights could, and should, be realised by working within the US Constitution. His goal was to ensure that the rhetoric of the **Bill of Rights** and the Declaration of Independence applied equally to all citizens. In order to achieve this, King was willing to work closely with the federal government, as well as Presidents Kennedy and Johnson.

King's vision was of a society in which black citizens were able to take a full part in and enjoy all the benefits of US culture. He wanted to integrate black people fully into US society. King's dream stood in stark contrast to Malcolm X's agenda, which claimed that US society was so corrupt that integration would be harmful to African-Americans.

Saint or sinner?

King was, and remains, a controversial figure. Questions about his effectiveness as a leader, his relationship with the white authorities, his ability to understand the difficulties faced by working-class African-Americans and his moral character dog his legacy.

King rose to national prominence during the Montgomery Bus Boycott of 1955–56. However, this boycott was initiated by local NAACP activists, and some NAACP members claimed that King effectively hijacked the campaign to further his own reputation. King faced similar criticisms from the leaders of the Greensboro sit-ins in 1960. In addition, King's poor organisational skills jeopardised the effectiveness of the SCLC's campaigns. It has been argued that, while King was highly effective at grabbing headlines and acting as a figurehead for the movement, he was poorly equipped to coordinate sustained local campaigns because his inspirational idealism was not allied with practical administrative skills. For example, the 1957 Crusade for Citizenship (an attempt to persuade federal government to guarantee voting rights for African-Americans) suffered as it was not supported by a sufficient number of salaried staff. In addition, the Chicago Campaign (1966) was accused of having no clear objectives and raising expectations that could not be met.

African-American leaders did not universally respect King. His refusal to sanction violent methods, the fact that he advocated 'turning the other cheek' and his sometimes close relationship with Presidents Kennedy and Johnson led some African-Americans to liken King to the fictional character **Uncle Tom**. They believed that King adopted a slavish attitude to the white authorities and that this was detrimental to the struggle of black Americans.

The strength of the accusation that King was an 'Uncle Tom' was increased by his perceived failure to understand the difficulties faced by working-class African-Americans. King's own relatively privileged background meant that he had never experienced many of the social and economic difficulties against which he campaigned. This was particularly pronounced during his northern campaigns. Furthermore, the majority of African-Americans in the northern states did not share King's Christian philosophy. This further underlined the differences between King and the people he sought to represent.

Finally, King was criticised for failing to live up to his Christian standards in his personal life. King had a series of affairs which some people saw as undermining his moral position.

However, while it is clear that King was no saint, he was undoubtedly an extraordinary individual. He possessed an ability to inspire black and white audiences through stirring oratory. He may not have experienced personally some of the oppression he fought, but he had the ability to articulate the feelings of many African-Americans. King's famous 'I Have a Dream' speech (1963) is a clear example of his outstanding ability as a speaker.

King managed to inspire with more than just words. His courage in the face of police brutality, racist violence and jail encouraged many activists to continue fighting. For instance, King stood firm when confronted by 30–40 threatening letters a day and when his own home was fire-bombed during the Montgomery Bus Boycott.

His ability to manipulate the media was perhaps King's greatest strength. Although he did not invent peaceful protest, King did realise that it was significantly more powerful in the age of mass media. The images of peaceful resistance to racist violence shocked the USA and brought public opinion behind King's campaigns. This technique was employed to great effect in Birmingham in 1963.

King's leadership was not without its critics. Nevertheless, his oratory, courage and ability to inspire made him the ideal figurehead for the Civil Rights movement, and his achievement was recognised in 1964 when he was awarded the Nobel Peace Prize.

Glossary

Bill of Rights — the first ten amendments to the US constitution, guaranteeing the rights of freedom of speech, assembly and conscience.

Uncle Tom — a fictional figure from the 1852 novel *Uncle Tom's Cabin* by Harriet Beecher Stowe, who was characterised by his devotion to his white owners. The term became an insult and was applied to Martin Luther King following his collaboration with Kennedy and Johnson.

Peaceful protest

Unity and disunity in the Civil Rights movement

The non-violent arm of the Civil Rights movement was made up of a variety of different groups, including the NAACP, CORE, SCLC and SNCC. Although the groups worked together successfully in a number of campaigns between 1945 and 1968, there were increasing tensions over their aims, methods and ideologies.

The NAACP and CORE were the oldest political groups fighting segregation. Their aims were broadly similar, but their methods were different. The NAACP's legal approach is discussed on page 20. The CORE, by contrast, was the first civil rights organisation to explore direct action, such as the sit-ins of the early 1960s. In this sense, the CORE was far more confrontational than the older, more conservative, NAACP.

In addition to the CORE, other groups embracing direct action were the SCLC and SNCC. The SCLC shared the NAACP's desire to work within the US system, and sought to work with it on public transport and voter registration issues. It deliberately refused to accept individual members, as this was part of the NAACP's strategy and it did not want to be seen as a rival organisation. The SNCC was formed in 1960 following the Greensboro sit-ins. It was different from the other groups as it focused on encouraging student participation in civil rights campaigns. From the start, the SNCC was more militant than the older organisations — its strategy was to provoke crisis situations deliberately, which would force action on the part of state and federal governments.

The year 1963 saw the establishment of the Coordinating Council of Community Organisations (CCCO). This brought the NAACP, CORE, SCLC and SNCC together in a joint campaign to further educational integration. The creation of the CCCO represented the high point of cooperation between the four groups.

However, in the months following the foundation of the CCCO, relations between the four groups began to deteriorate. By 1963 the NAACP's legal campaign appeared to have run its course and the focus of the Civil Rights movement in general shifted to demands for *de facto* change. Consequently, direct action was seen as a more appropriate method and the NAACP's influence declined.

After 1964, the CORE turned to more militant campaigns for employment rights in the northern states. Its change of tactic stemmed from the realisation that its peaceful campaigns had helped only middle-class black citizens — militancy was seen as a way of helping the black working class. This sometimes violent militancy marked a divergence from the SCLC, which remained committed to exclusively peaceful methods.

The SNCC also distanced itself deliberately from the SCLC, to counter the perception that it was essentially the student wing of King's organisation. Between 1961 and 1964, the SNCC focused on non-violent direct action to achieve integration. This included sit-ins and voter registration campaigns (1964). The year 1964 was a turning point for the SNCC, when its efforts to establish the Mississippi Freedom Democratic Party were vetoed by the Democratic National Convention. Following this, the SNCC refused to work in coalition with white people and advocated black separatism rather than racial integration. The SNCC also emphasised the importance of local grass-roots activism, and its strategy was to encourage black people to organise themselves. In this sense it was different from the SCLC, which it believed to be composed of members of the middle-class black elite, who tended to impose their organisation and strategies on the communities in which they worked. In 1966, the SNCC published a position paper in the *New York Times* which openly criticised the SCLC and the NAACP as well as stating that white people had no further role in the black movement.

In the late 1960s, peaceful protest was increasingly eclipsed by militant groups who claimed that non-violent protest was incapable of improving conditions for African-Americans.

What did peaceful protest achieve?

Direct action helped to change the law and was used to test the implementation of these laws. During the Montgomery Bus Boycott (1956), the Greensboro sit-ins (1960) and the Birmingham campaign (1963), direct action proved particularly successful at winning public support for the civil rights cause. Peaceful protest gave activists the moral high ground. This was especially evident in Birmingham, where media coverage contrasted the brutality of the white police with the dignity of the black protesters. The shift in public opinion helped to convince local and federal law makers that change was necessary. Peaceful protest achieved the destruction of 'Jim Crow' laws in a number of major cities in the southern states.

Aside from changing the law, peaceful protest also sought to test the law. For example, during the Freedom Rides (1961), the aim of the non-violent direct action was to realise the legal gains of the NAACP campaigns, thus bringing about *de facto* change out of

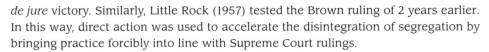

de jure victory. Similarly, Little Rock (1957) tested the Brown ruling of 2 years earlier. In this way, direct action was used to accelerate the disintegration of segregation by bringing practice forcibly into line with Supreme Court rulings.

The cumulative effect of peaceful protest in the early 1960s helped to create the public support and political will to enact the Civil Rights Act (1964) and the Voting Rights Act (1965). These acts had national significance and underlined the effectiveness of non-violent campaigning.

Peaceful protest was not always successful. It came to rely increasingly on provoking a violent response from overzealous white authorities. In cases where the local authorities were shrewd and refused to be provoked, little change was evident. Albany (1961), for example, failed to effect any meaningful change for precisely this reason.

Non-violent direct action essentially failed to bring about social and economic change. King's Chicago Campaign (1966) achieved nothing more than vague promises from Chicago's mayor Richard Daley. King acknowledged that effecting social and economic change was necessarily harder than challenging segregation, as the former was both costly and not simply a matter of changing the law.

Even after the Selma campaign (1965) and the Voting Rights Act of 1965, the proportion of black citizens registered to vote never equalled the proportion of registered white voters. By the end of 1966, four out of the 13 southern states still had fewer than 50% of its African-Americans registered to vote.

Federal government

Civil rights campaigners often looked to federal government to advance their cause — 'Jim Crow' laws were peculiar to the southern states and could be overruled by federal bodies. During the period 1945–68 there were four US presidents, Truman, Eisenhower, Kennedy and Johnson, who each played a part in the development of the Civil Rights movement.

Harry S. Truman (1945–53)

As a senator in the early 1940s, Truman publicly opposed lynching and declared himself a believer in the brotherhood of men, regardless of race. In 1946, Truman established a committee to investigate violence against African-Americans. The committee's report, *To Secure These Rights* (1947), recommended anti-lynching legislation, desegregation of interstate transport and the armed forces, and federal support for civil rights lawsuits, as well as the founding of the United States Commission on Civil Rights. Truman accepted the findings of this report and issued an executive order to end discrimination in the armed forces and the civil service. He also endeavoured to open more public housing to African-Americans after 1948. In doing so, he faced opposition from Congress, his own party and the top officials in the military. Nonetheless, Truman set a precedent for presidential concern with civil rights.

Truman's interest was in part due to political necessity. Although he still used racist terminology in private, Truman was careful not to use it in public. He was aware that, in the northern states at least, the Democrats needed the black vote. What is more, Truman was a determined 'cold warrior' who knew that the USA could never be presented as the land of the free while overt racial discrimination continued unchallenged within its borders.

However, political necessity cannot completely explain Truman's concern with civil rights. He may have gained two-thirds of the black vote in the 1948 presidential election, but his stance on civil rights alienated many southern Democrats who were traditionally the core of the Democrat vote. Fundamentally, Truman was motivated by a desire to modernise the USA. He believed that segregation was bad for the economy and left the USA 80 years behind the rest of the world.

Dwight D. Eisenhower (1953–61)

Eisenhower's presidency spanned several major events in the civil rights campaign, such as the Brown cases, the Montgomery Bus Boycott, the Little Rock campaign, the Greensboro sit-ins and the Freedom Rides. However, Eisenhower had little sympathy with these campaigns and met with Martin Luther King and other black leaders only once. He refused to give federal support to the Montgomery Bus Boycott and, until the events of Little Rock, declined to use federal power to enforce the Brown decision. Broadly speaking, Eisenhower took the view that race relations would improve of their own accord over time.

The exceptions to Eisenhower's hands-off approach were the Civil Rights Acts of 1957 and 1960. Eisenhower proposed legislation to guarantee the vote to all citizens and to establish a special division of the Justice Department to deal with civil rights. However, when Democratic senators attacked the **bill**, Eisenhower backed down. Consequently, the 1957 Civil Rights Act was watered down significantly — for example, the **act** specified that white officials who denied black citizens the right to vote could be tried by all-white juries. When Eisenhower passed a second bill in 1960, it infuriated southern senators again and Eisenhower failed to give the bill his wholehearted support. His two Civil Rights Acts added a mere 3% of black voters to the electoral rolls by the end of 1960.

Eisenhower was reluctant to show clear leadership on issues relating to civil rights because he was aware that it could lose him the support of white voters. Moreover, he had been born and raised in the segregated south, and he shared the assumptions of many white racists. He regarded the activities of groups such as the SCLC as unduly aggressive and sympathised with white southerners who felt threatened by civil rights campaigns.

Eisenhower's motivation for proposing the civil rights bills was in fact the impending presidential elections. His goal was to win the black vote without alienating the southern white vote. This motivation goes some way to explaining why the 1957 and 1960 bills promised much but delivered little.

John F. Kennedy (1961–63)

During his presidential campaign Kennedy pledged to help African-American citizens, because he believed racism to be a moral evil. Kennedy's phone call to Coretta King in 1960, while her husband was in prison, did much to convince black voters that Kennedy was sympathetic to their cause. Once in office, however, he took no immediate action, concentrating instead on legislation to improve healthcare and decrease poverty. Kennedy was concerned that focusing on civil rights would alienate southern congressmen and jeopardise his healthcare and poverty legislation, so the action he did take on civil rights was mainly symbolic. For example, he appointed five black federal judges, including the NAACP's chief council Thurgood Marshall, and he invited more African-Americans to the White House than any previous president. Additionally, he created the Committee on Equal Employment Opportunity (CEEO), which was mandated to ensure equal employment opportunities for the employees of the federal government. However, the success of the CEEO was easy to exaggerate — an increase from one to two black employees in a government office could be presented as a 100% increase in the employment of African-Americans by that office.

Kennedy's sympathies for civil rights broadly followed public opinion. In the late 1950s, he opposed Eisenhower's civil rights bills for political reasons. However, as the public became increasingly interested in civil rights issues, Kennedy's attitude softened. Essentially, he was reluctant to show leadership on civil rights issues.

The success of civil rights campaigns forced President Kennedy to take action. He refused to press for an end to segregation in Birmingham, Alabama until King's campaign had provoked public outrage at the treatment of African-Americans in the city. Kennedy's approach to civil rights legislation was typical of his general attitude to the movement. He committed himself to a civil rights bill during his election campaign, but took no action until June 1963. Even then, the March on Washington was necessary to persuade Kennedy to make the bill a priority. For these reasons, by the end of 1963 Kennedy was prepared to risk his political career and support the bill.

Lyndon B. Johnson (1963–69)

Johnson became president following the assassination of Kennedy in November 1963. During the 1950s, Johnson was a firm supporter of the Supreme Court's rulings on the

Brown cases and later orchestrated the passing of Eisenhower's Civil Rights Acts. As president, Johnson was committed fully to passing the Civil Rights Act (1964) — he went as far as to say that he would sacrifice his chance of re-election if this were necessary to pass the act, and he collaborated publicly with Martin Luther King on this bill and the Voting Rights Act of 1965. Although the success of the 1964 act has been attributed to Kennedy's campaign and public sympathy following Kennedy's death, it was in fact Johnson's tireless agitation in the Senate that ensured the bill's success. Following the Selma campaign, Johnson also proposed and ensured the passage of the Voting Rights Act (1965).

Johnson's commitment to civil rights was also evident in his educational reforms. The Elementary and Secondary Education Act (1965) and the Higher Education Act (1965) increased the funding set aside for education provision in poorer states. This led to the quadrupling of black college students between 1965 and 1975. Furthermore, Johnson's 1968 Civil Rights Act sought to outlaw racial discrimination in the housing market.

Johnson was committed ideologically to a vision of the USA as the 'Great Society', and an end to racism was at the heart of this vision. He claimed that 'the Great Society rests on abundance and liberty for all. It demands an end to poverty and racial injustice, to which we are totally committed in our time.' He was aware that legislation alone could not secure equality and that 'affirmative action' was needed before African-Americans could be truly equal.

Johnson's measures met opposition from Congress, as well as from state authorities. Additionally, the increased militancy of the civil rights campaigners increased white opposition to further reform. Finally, the Vietnam War (1965–73) removed both funding and attention from the campaign for civil rights. Nonetheless, Johnson undoubtedly achieved more than any of his predecessors in advancing the cause of racial equality.

Congress and the Supreme Court

Congress, the USA's supreme law-making body, played a significant role in advancing African-American rights from 1945 to 1968. Initially, Congress resisted legal changes in favour of African-Americans. For example, Eisenhower's attempts to pass the Civil Rights Act (1957) were hampered severely by Congressmen from both parties. Southern senators opposed the bill as they feared the major changes it would cause in their segregated constituencies. One congressional strategy used to defeat the bill was to table a series of amendments that would weaken it, but even the weakened act was more than some southern senators were prepared to endorse. For example, South Carolina's Senator J. Strom Thurmond spoke in Congress for 24 hours and 18 minutes against the bill. Although this technique of talking until a bill runs out of congressional time (known as a filibuster) failed, the bill was so weakened that it achieved little for African-Americans.

However, by the mid-1960s Congress was prepared to pass a series of important acts. For example, 73 of the 100 senators and 289 of the 435 members of the House of Representatives voted in favour of the Civil Rights Act of 1964. Similarly, the 1968 Civil Rights Act was passed with 71 votes in the Senate and 250 votes in the House of Representatives. However, there remained strong opposition from southern members of the House of Representatives — all 10 of its southern Republican members and 87 of its 94 southern Democrat members voted against the 1964 act. Although the majority of Congress was in favour of legal change, its conservative members remained consistently opposed to increased rights for African-Americans.

The Supreme Court was also a significant factor in overturning segregation. Early NAACP campaigns focused almost exclusively on the Supreme Court in its battle to challenge segregation legally; from the mid-1940s, the NAACP fought a series of campaigns to persuade the Supreme Court that segregation was unconstitutional. Between 1954 and 1960, the Supreme Court made a series of landmark judgements that paved the way for the Civil Rights Act of 1964, and the consequent end to segregation in the southern states.

In 1953, President Eisenhower appointed Earl Warren as Chief Justice of the Supreme Court. Warren's sympathy for the plight of African-Americans was evident in cases such as Brown, Brown II and *Browder* v *Gayle*, which marked the beginning of the end for segregation. Warren's impact was such that Eisenhower later remarked that his appointment 'was the biggest damned fool mistake I've ever made in my life'.

Glossary

act of Congress — a law that is passed by both houses of the US Congress and ratified by the president.

bill — a proposal that is put before Congress for approval.

Malcolm X and Black Power

Explaining the emergence of Black Power

Black Power was attractive to many African-Americans because of the perceived short-comings of the non-violent Civil Rights movement, the general radicalisation of US culture in the 1960s and the shift in focus of the Civil Rights movement from south to north.

By 1965, peaceful protest had brought about considerable *de jure* change. Nonetheless, black people throughout the USA still experienced informal discrimination. At the same time, federal government and white opinion were no longer as sympathetic to issues of civil rights. Many white people believed that the Civil Rights Act (1964) and the Voting

Rights Act (1965) marked the end of legitimate demands for reform. Additionally, the Vietnam War became the focus of white liberal protest and highlighted the dangers of radicalism to conservatives, as well as occupying much of President Johnson's time. For these reasons, many young black Americans turned to more radical methods of protest.

The 1960s witnessed a general cultural liberalisation among students and young people. This was evident in new attitudes to sexual relationships, hallucinogenic drugs and psychedelic music culture. Young people became more interested in experimental and even revolutionary lifestyles. From this perspective, the older branches of the Civil Rights movements, such as the NAACP and the SCLC, were seen as too conservative, committed as they were to working with the establishment. Younger people also believed that the Vietnam War and continuing racial discrimination indicated that the establishment was fundamentally corrupt and that revolutionary change was needed.

Divisions within the Civil Rights movement contributed to black militancy. When an assassination attempt was made on James Meredith during his 1966 'March Against Fear', other members of the movement continued the march in his name, but with a newly radical tone. Meredith's original intention had been to use the march to encourage black voter registration across the southern states. However, after he was shot, leading members of the SNCC continued the march with a more radical agenda, chanting 'Black Power! Black Power!' and using the symbol of the clenched fist. Furthermore, the SNCC wanted to exclude white participants from the march, and Stokely Carmichael encouraged violence towards property by advocating the burning of every courthouse in Mississippi. The march marked a turning point in the relationship between the SNCC, the SCLC and the NAACP. Martin Luther King was concerned about this new direction — he felt that it would provoke a white backlash and jeopardise hopes of further reform. These divisions led to polarisation within the movement, and King was no longer able to exert any influence over the radicals in the SNCC — their militancy was able to continue unchecked.

King's non-violent methods seemed to be increasingly irrelevant, especially in the northern campaigns of the 1960s. For example, the Chicago Campaign (1966) achieved little more than a paper victory. Moreover, when the SCLC was given a government grant of $4 million to help improve ghetto housing, local African-Americans claimed that the government had bought off King and the SCLC, which discredited King further. Many African-Americans in the northern states felt forced to look elsewhere for a movement that would truly represent them.

Radicals such as Malcolm X appealed to black Americans in the late 1960s because of their uncompromising message. Unlike King, they rejected any alliance with the white citizens or the 'white government'. Consequently, it could never be claimed that someone such as Malcolm X was 'a tool of the white man'. Moreover, Malcolm X had been brought up in a northern working-class environment, so he was seen to understand better the position of northern African-Americans. Malcolm X's advocacy of the use of violence as self-defence was viewed increasingly as the only viable response to white violence.

Achievements of Black Power

Legal change was never the goal of the Black Power movement. Consequently, the absence of a body of legislation comparable to the Civil Rights Acts and Voting Rights Act cannot be construed as a failure on its part, because the Black Power movement certainly had an influence. For example, Martin Luther King could not ignore its rhetoric and spoke increasingly in terms of 'Black Pride' and 'revolution rather than reform'. Groups such as the Black Panthers kept the economic position of black Americans on the political agenda through their Ten-Point Program, and Black Power inspired a new confidence in black culture. For example, in the late 1960s the jazz musician Miles Davis started working almost exclusively with other black musicians and deliberately stressed African influences in his musical style.

What had been achieved by 1968?

The year 1968 was a turning point for the Civil Rights movement. It witnessed the assassination of Martin Luther King, the election of the conservative Richard Nixon as US president and the imprisonment of Bobby Seale and Huey P. Newton (co-founders of the Black Panther Party). By 1968, enormous gains had been made by the movement, although the majority of African-Americans still faced poverty and discrimination.

Gains: 1945–68

The Civil Rights Act (1964) was the culmination of postwar campaigns for social and economic racial equality. The act banned segregation across the USA and gave federal government the power to enforce this ban. By late 1965, 214 cities had desegregated formally and the proportion of black children in segregated schools had decreased substantially. More opportunities in education, coupled with the increase of fair employment practices, led to the rise of a black middle class. By 1969, over a third of black households had a combined annual income of at least $10,000.

Politically, the Voting Rights Act (1965) consolidated and extended the gains made by previous campaigns and legal cases, such as Smith v Allwright (1944) and the Mississippi Freedom Summer (the SNCC's voter registration campaign of 1964). The act outlawed explicitly any state legislation that barred black people from voting, whatever the pretext, and its impact was immediate and major. By 1968 there were over 3 million registered black voters in the southern states, and by 1970 1,400 black people had been elected to public office. Moreover, the impact of black voters was evident in the sharp decline of candidates in the south representing the major parties that publicly supported segregation. Finally, the state governors in the north responded to the demands of black voters by appointing black people to senior positions in their administrations. The New York Governor Nelson Rockefeller and Mayor John V. Lindsay both increased their share of the black vote following the appointment of high-profile black individuals.

Another notable change was the increased white support for racial equality which took place from 1945 to 1968, especially in the media. One significant example was the inclusion of a black character in the popular science-fiction series *Star Trek*, as part of the racially mixed crew of the Starship Enterprise. In 1966, the programme featured the first interracial kiss to be screened on US television. Similarly, during the 1960s black recording artists such as Miles Davis began to insist that black models appeared on their album covers. This trend was also evident in printed media — the *Wall Street Journal*, *Time* magazine and the *New Yorker* frequently ran articles supporting the campaign for civil rights.

The gains of the Civil Rights movement took place for a number of reasons. The civil rights campaigns were instrumental in focusing public and government attention on racial inequalities, and they led to the emergence of black leaders who were able to act as figureheads for the movement and negotiate with federal government.

The increasing willingness of federal government to address formal inequalities can be partly explained by the emergence of strong leaders for the movement. However, the Kennedy and Johnson administrations were also committed ideologically to ending formal discrimination, and in Johnson's case his vision of the 'Great Society' aimed to tackle poverty for all Americans.

The Cold War ensured that racial integration was made a federal issue. President Truman in particular saw the paradox of condemning Soviet tyranny and allowing the oppression of African-Americans to continue in the USA.

The NAACP was able to demonstrate successfully to the Supreme Court that segregation was unconstitutional. This reflected a greater liberalism in the Supreme Court's outlook than was evident prior to the Second World War.

Finally, the media played a crucial role in drawing the civil rights campaign to the attention of a wider public, and in increasing support for its goals. Moreover, the media brought figures such as Martin Luther King to national prominence, reflected to the federal government a public desire for change and provided further impetus for reform by showing the inequity of segregation to a global audience.

The limits of progress by 1968

In spite of the success of the Voting Rights Act (1965), black citizens were still marginalised politically in the USA. A smaller proportion of black people than white people were registered to vote — for example, 77% of white voters in the northern states were registered, whereas only 71% of black voters were registered. The situation was worse in the southern states, where 71% of white Americans were registered, compared with only 62% of black Americans. Furthermore, many southern states elected no black representatives, and many of the appointments made by white politicians in the northern states were seen as tokenistic. Indeed, the majority of black appointments were made without consulting black voters, and those appointed were usually given jobs in race relations. It is worth noting that in the 1968 presidential election, Richard Nixon was successful by appealing to southern white voters rather than attempting to engage black voters.

Progress on social and economic issues was also slow. Black ghettos, with inadequate housing and educational facilities, were still a feature of many northern cities. In 1968, only two northern states had commissions that enforced fair treatment in housing and employment. Similarly, in the southern states *de facto* segregation continued, particularly in the areas of education and employment. Indeed, 58% of black southerners sent their children to segregated schools in 1968.

The limits of progress can be explained, in part, by continuing prejudice among many white Americans. The legal changes won by the Civil Rights movement did not weaken the antagonism of racist whites. Racism was not confined to the southern states — President Johnson's Kerner Commission demonstrated this in its report of 1967, by attributing the northern ghetto riots to white racism. In the southern states, racist state governors continued to be elected, reflecting ongoing racial prejudice on the part of their white constituents. For example, in 1966, a year after the Voting Rights Act (1965) was passed, Lurleen Wallace was elected governor of Alabama because of her commitment to maintaining segregated schools. In 1970, her husband, George C. Wallace, was elected on a similar platform.

But the prejudice of white Americans was not the only factor inhibiting progress. Other factors included the federal government's preoccupation with the Vietnam War, the breakdown of the civil rights coalition following the rise of Black Power, the reaction of white opinion to this increased radicalisation and the economic nature of the remaining problems.

The Vietnam War had a major impact on the success of the Civil Rights movement. First, the war distracted President Johnson from his domestic agenda. Second, it created division between Martin Luther King and President Johnson, following King's criticism of US involvement. Third, the war polarised US public opinion, tending to heighten the conservatism and nationalism (and therefore racism) on the right and radicalism on the left.

After 1965, the Civil Rights movement lost its cohesion. The radicalisation of the CORE and the SNCC meant that collaboration between these groups and the SCLC became unviable. These divisions reduced the authority of black leaders as they could no longer claim to speak for the whole of black America. Furthermore, the militancy of the Black Panthers, the SNCC and the CORE provoked a backlash among white liberals — there was no longer a multiracial coalition seeking further integration. Black militancy also provided white racists with evidence that black people were 'an enemy within the United States' — a point of particular sensitivity as the USA was at war in Vietnam at the time. J. Edgar Hoover, head of the FBI, made this very point when he argued that the Black Panthers were 'the greatest threat to the internal security of the country'.

Finally, Martin Luther King argued that further change would be more difficult because the remaining problems facing black Americans were economic rather than legal. King suggested that once the emancipation of African-Americans started to affect white people financially, they would lose sympathy with the cause. Indeed, the kind of economic change that King's Poor People's Campaign (1968) proposed was opposed by powerful vested interests — for example, US business leaders.

Questions
&
Answers

In this section there are five specimen exam questions. Two specimen answers are given to each question: an A-grade and a C-grade response. All the specimen answers are the subject of detailed examiner comments, preceded by the icon **e**. These should be studied carefully because they show how and why marks are awarded or lost.

When exam papers are marked, all answers are given a level of response and then a precise numerical mark. Answers to questions worth 20 marks are normally marked according to three levels:
- **level 1:** 1–6 marks
- **level 2:** 7–16 marks
- **level 3:** 17–20 marks

Answers to questions worth 40 marks are marked according to four levels:
- **level 1:** 1–8 marks
- **level 2:** 9–20 marks
- **level 3:** 21–35 marks
- **level 4:** 36–40 marks

Question 1

(a) What were the key features of the Black Power movement in the 1960s? (20 marks)

(b) Why was progress towards racial equality so slow in the years 1945–55? (40 marks)

Total: 60 marks

■ ■ ■

A-grade answer

(a) The Black Power movement came to prominence in the USA in the 1960s. Although the term is used to describe a number of different groups that lack a coherent ideology, common beliefs and attitudes can be recognised within the movement.

This introduction gives a focused summary to the essay. It addresses the question and goes on to sketch out the different areas that the essay will explore.

First, Black Power groups believed that black Americans had the right to defend themselves against white violence. For example, the Black Panthers (founded in 1966) were an armed self-defence force who patrolled black areas in the USA specifically to defend African-Americans from racist white police. Similarly, Malcolm X encouraged African-Americans to own guns — owning guns and using them in self-defence was legal. Therefore, the Black Power movement can be distinguished from the Civil Rights movement as a whole because it rejected the non-violent ideals of Martin Luther King.

This is a well-structured paragraph. The first sentence addresses the question directly, and the candidate offers two examples to prove the point made. The paragraph finishes with a sentence showing how the point and examples answer the question. This is a level 3 response.

Second, the Black Power movement was in favour of self-determination, the right to govern oneself. In the context of Black Power, this meant Black Nationalism — black people taking control of their own destiny. The SNCC expelled white members from its organisation, as it believed that it was up to black people to organise their own campaigns. The SNCC and the Nation of Islam also believed in a separate state for black people, as a white majority would always oppress a black minority in the USA. In this way, Black Power's call for separatism was different from the NAACP and the SCLC's campaigns for integration.

Third, the Black Power groups were united in their desire to improve the social and economic status of black Americans. This is clear in the activities of the Black Panthers, such as the Free Breakfast for School Children Program, which provided food for 10,000 children daily by the late 1960s. Malcolm X also advocated that black people achieve economic success through self-help. This focus on *de facto* change distinguished Black Power from the NAACP and SCLC, who were more interested in legal (*de jure*) change.

In spite of these similarities, Black Power was never a coherent movement and many of its aims were not clear. For example, there was no clear programme for the creation of a black state or economic improvement. Perhaps this incoherence was the final feature of Black Power.

> 🖉 **This is an excellent essay. It answers the question clearly by considering three relevant factors, and gives a lot of detail and explicit explanation. The conclusion brings together the previous points and draws out the implication that Black Power was not a unified movement, which summarises and extends the scope of the essay.**

Level 3: 20/20

(b) Progress towards racial equality was slow between 1945 and 1955 for a number of reasons. These include the lack of wholehearted support from federal government, the absence of organised protest, the lack of a spokesperson for black people, the limits of the NAACP's campaign, public opinion and the absence of media attention.

> 🖉 This is a focused introduction that outlines the structure of the rest of the essay.

Between 1945 and 1955, US Presidents Truman and Eisenhower were either unsympathetic to or distracted from advancing civil rights. Although Truman brought in a number of measures to help African-Americans (such as desegregating the army), he also knew that his party was dependent on the votes of racist whites in the southern states. The end of his presidency was spent dealing with the Korean War, which distracted him from further moves towards desegregation. Eisenhower, on the other hand, was unsympathetic to the plight of black people. He thought that they were aggressive and ungrateful for their position in the USA and he therefore failed to enforce the Brown decision of 1954. Without federal support, it was very difficult for civil rights campaigners to achieve their goals — federal government was the only agency able to enforce civil rights policy across the whole of the USA.

> 🖉 This paragraph makes a point, backs it up with specific examples and explains its relevance to the question. This is an excellent structure which is replicated throughout the essay.

There was no coherent mass protest between 1945 and 1955. In the 1960s, the movement achieved notable success in challenging Jim Crow laws owing to its high profile and organised mass campaigns. In the late 1940s and early 1950s, however, challenges to segregation were mostly legal. Examples of this are the NAACP's case challenging segregation in interstate travel (*Morgan* v *Virginia*, 1946) and the Brown case of 1954, which challenged segregation in schools. These campaigns failed to advance the cause significantly, because they did not attract the same media attention that mass action would do a decade later.

The campaign was also slow because of the lack of a black figurehead. The absence of a leader such as Martin Luther King meant that there was nobody to speak on behalf of the black community to the media or to federal government. Equally, there was no unifying figure to rally black support for the fight against Jim Crow laws. The absence of a focal point made progress slow, as mass black dissatisfaction could not be turned into change.

Throughout this period the racism of many whites remained unaltered. Groups such as the KKK influenced opinion in the southern states. In the northern states the existence of black ghettos prevented racial integration and therefore hindered the acceptance of African-Americans as equals. Progress was slow because there simply was not the public support that was necessary before change could happen.

The NAACP's focus on legal change, the absence of a charismatic black leader, and the fact that the media were dominated by white people meant that the media were not interested in the struggle for equality during this period. For example, despite its importance, the Brown case failed to attract substantial media coverage, which meant that the majority of Americans remained ignorant of the injustices of segregation and of the anti-segregation campaign. The absence of media coverage explains the limited progress towards equality, because without publicity it was difficult to increase support for the movement.

🖉 The beginning of this paragraph demonstrates how the different factors discussed in the essay are interlinked. This substantiated explanation ensures that the essay would be awarded level 4.

In essence, progress was slow between 1945 and 1955 because the campaigns of this period lacked many of the characteristics that made later campaigns so successful. Without federal support, media attention, a charismatic leader and the development of mass protest, the movement was unable to gain the public sympathy necessary to advance racial equality in the USA.

🖉 **This is a fine essay. The factors discussed demonstrate detailed knowledge of a range of issues, and there is an explanatory focus on the question throughout. In addition, the candidate shows understanding of how the factors have combined to produce the end result. However, this answer would have achieved a higher mark if the integration had occurred throughout the essay rather than simply in the conclusion.**

Level 4: 37/40

Total: 57/60

■ ■ ■

C-grade answer

(a) In the 1940s and 1950s, there were many legal battles which resulted in *de jure* victories such as Brown, Brown II and *Sweatt* v *Painter*. Until 1965 there were many direct action campaigns such as Albany and the Freedom Rides organised by groups such as the SCLC and the SNCC. Black Power is different as it came about in the late 1960s.

@ Most of the information in this introduction does not address the question. Although the candidate attempts to give some historical background here, it is not made relevant to the question. However, the final sentence does address the question directly, albeit in a simplistic fashion.

Black Power is also different because unlike the SCLC and Martin Luther King, the leaders of the Black Power movement did not support non-violence fully. Black Power leaders were influenced by revolutionaries who were prepared to use violence, e.g. Mao Zedong, Che Guevara and by Robert Williams's book, *Negroes with Guns*. Malcolm X is another example. He called Martin Luther King's non-violence a 'philosophy of the fool'.

@ This paragraph offers some relevant detail, but there is no attempt to link it to the question. This is a common mistake that prevents candidates from achieving above level 2.

The Black Panther Party was socialist as well as Black Nationalist and supported economic and social equality for African-Americans. It wanted class unity and criticised middle-class African-Americans who were not united with working-class African-Americans. Malcolm X also became a socialist towards the end of his life after he went on his pilgrimage to Mecca and decided that some of his views were too extreme. Shortly after this he was shot. Stokely Carmichael's book *Stokely Speaks* also has socialist ideas in it.

@ There is relevant information in this paragraph, but the candidate does not answer the question explicitly. This paragraph would be better focused on the question if it began with a sentence that stated that Black Power groups were often inspired by socialism.

Martin Luther King was also criticised by Black Power's leaders. The SNCC broke with the SCLC and King, calling him an 'Uncle Tom', meaning he was a white man's tool. Malcolm X said that Martin Luther King's dream was in fact a nightmare and that there was nothing good about black people and white people sharing the same toilets. The Black Panthers also thought that Martin Luther King was making too many compromises with whites such as with Presidents Johnson and Kennedy.

In conclusion, the most important feature of Black Power was its criticism of Martin Luther King for being an 'Uncle Tom'.

@ This conclusion does not add anything to the essay. Although it asserts that one of the factors discussed in the essay is more important than the others, it does not show why this is the case. The examiner cannot therefore credit this comment.

@ **This essay is a strong level 2 answer. There is generally a good focus on the question, with three developed statements and one statement with weaker development. There are, however, some irrelevant parts — for example, the statement 'Shortly after this he was shot' adds nothing to the point that**

Malcolm X was influenced by socialism. If the candidate had ended each paragraph with a sentence explaining how the paragraph answered the question, the essay would have been awarded a mark in level 3.

Level 2: 15/20

(b) Many African-Americans faced discrimination and racial inequality in 1945. In the southern states there was legal discrimination through Jim Crow laws such as grandfather clauses, and in the northern states many African-Americans lived in ghettos. The government supported this to an extent and segregated the army. For example, black people had one mess hall and white people had another. In 1945 the position of black people was bad and a lot of progress was needed.

This introduction does not address the question — it simply describes the background to the question.

The NAACP was a group that helped to fight problems such as the Jim Crow laws. It used legal methods and took the government to court over education and transport to try to get some change. This was a slow process because the courts were not sympathetic to black issues. The court cases took a long time because there were many courts to pass through before a case reached the Supreme Court, where a final decision was made. Even when it did make a decision, it was sometimes so vague that the NAACP had to fight the case all over again.

The focus of this paragraph is better, but it lacks detailed development.

The presidents were also not much help. Truman desegregated the armed forces and commissioned a report. The report showed that there was a lot of progress to be made before black people were equal to white people. President Eisenhower's acts were not very helpful. He passed a Civil Rights Act, but this was opposed by important white politicians. It was not effective when it was finally passed, because the white politicians had changed it.

Again, the support for the point in this paragraph is too generalised.

White people were still racist and they did not want change. Many people in important positions were racists. The Ku Klux Klan still had a lot of power and tried to stop change happening. It was very successful and this explains why change was slow between 1945 and 1955.

Although this contains an explanatory link to the question, the lack of supporting evidence makes it little more than an unsubstantiated assertion.

Many black people did not have the vote in the southern states because of grandfather clauses, so they could not vote for change — therefore change was slow in the years 1945 to 1955. This kept black people out of power, so white racists like the KKK could run the government in the southern states.

Because black people received worse education than white people, they were not able to get into good jobs or positions of power. Therefore, there were few black people in the media and so the media was not interested in black problems. Lack of media interest meant that progress towards racial equality was slow in the years 1945 to 1955.

Progress was slow because of many factors such as white racism and the grand-father clauses.

e This conclusion is extremely weak — it does not summarise the points made in the essay.

e This answer focuses on the question throughout and discusses a range of factors. However, there is a lack of detailed supporting information and almost no specific supporting examples are provided. Furthermore, there are no developed explanatory links. This answer would be improved by including references to specific events (e.g. *Brown* v *Board of Education*, 1954) and by evaluating their effectiveness (e.g. the fact that only 3% of black voters were added to the electoral roll following Eisenhower's Civil Rights Act).

Level 2: 20/40

Total: 35/60

Question 2

(a) **What steps did the NAACP take to challenge 'Jim Crow' laws in the decade following the Second World War?** (20 marks)

(b) **Why was the Civil Rights Act of 1964 passed?** (40 marks)

Total: 60 marks

■ ■ ■

A-grade answer

(a) In the decade following the Second World War, the NAACP focused on achieving change through legal methods. Its campaigns concerned transport and education.

The NAACP's strategy was to challenge 'Jim Crow' laws through the courts. Essentially, it aimed to prove that local laws segregating education and transport were unconstitutional. The NAACP had already had some success with this legal strategy in the case *Smith* v *Allwright* (1944), which established that the 15th Amendment applied to primary elections and that therefore black people had the right to vote in primaries in Texas. All of the steps taken by the NAACP to challenge 'Jim Crow' laws followed this pattern and were legal in nature.

e This paragraph concerns the strategy of the NAACP and is therefore relevant to the question. However, the example of *Smith* v *Allwright* took place in 1944 — this is outside of the range of the question.

The NAACP's campaign to desegregate education consisted of three steps. First, *Sweatt* v *Painter* in 1950 ruled that black people must receive the same level of education as white people — this overturned *Plessy* v *Ferguson*, which had ruled that black and white people could receive separate education as long as it was equal. In 1954, the Brown case attempted to apply this to a specific school in Topeka. Although the NAACP won this case, the court ruling did not specify a timetable for the desegregation of schools. Therefore, in 1955, the NAACP took the third step, known as Brown II, in which the Supreme Court ruled that desegregation in education should proceed 'with all deliberate speed'. In this sense, the NAACP's first step was to establish the principle, the second step was to apply the principle to a specific school, and the third step was designed to secure a legal timetable for desegregation in education.

e This paragraph is excellent. It addresses the question directly, contains sound development and clear explanation, and focuses consistently on the idea of 'steps'.

In the area of transport, the NAACP fought *Morgan* v *Virginia* in 1946. This case established that segregation on interstate travel was illegal. This was the first step in a process that led to *Browder* v *Gayle* (1956), which attempted to apply the principle of this ruling to local transport in Montgomery, and then to *Boynton* v *Virginia* (1960), which extended the principle of *Morgan* v *Virginia* to travel terminals.

By 1955, the NAACP had taken legal steps to establish that segregation was unconstitutional in the areas of education and interstate transport. This was a significant step towards full desegregation.

> **This question focuses on the 'steps' taken by the NAACP. By breaking down the NAACP's campaign into stages, the candidate writes a focused thematic answer that addresses the question directly. However, the answer addresses only two relevant factors, as the second paragraph deals with a case outside the period specified in the question. This response would receive a low level 3 — although it has an explanatory focus, it only deals with a limited number of factors.**

Level 3: 18/20

(b) The 1964 Civil Rights Act is often seen as the climax of the postwar civil rights campaigns. It would not have come about had it not been for the unity of the Civil Rights movement and the March on Washington, as well as the sympathetic media and public. Individuals also had their roles to play — these included Presidents Kennedy and Johnson, and Martin Luther King.

> **This introduction is punchy and impressive. It demonstrates an understanding of the importance of the topic and outlines a thematic approach to the question.**

The early 1960s witnessed a significant degree of unity between different civil rights groups. At this time, the SCLC, SNCC, CORE and NAACP were all committed to integration through non-violent means. For example, the SCLC was formed during the Montgomery Bus Boycott and the SNCC during the spontaneous sit-ins in Greensboro. This unity of aims and methods, coupled with the successes of these non-violent protests, led to legal change in 1964 as the movement increased the pressure on federal government for substantial change.

Popular support for the Civil Rights Act was crucial to its success. Increasing white support for the Civil Rights movement was evident in the sit-ins, the Montgomery Bus Boycott and the Freedom Rides. The popularity of radical measures with white people was important for the passing of the Civil Rights Act, because Kennedy's administration lacked a popular mandate and Kennedy was unwilling to take bold steps that did not enjoy public support.

The media were also influential in winning public support for the act — broadcasts of Bull Connor's violence towards protesters in Birmingham in 1963 shocked domestic and world audiences. Additionally, in 1963, US magazines such as the *Wall Street Journal*, *Newsweek* and *Life* all ran articles supporting racial integration. The media's role was significant because it increased the pressure for change from both within and outside the USA.

e This paragraph has a strong explanatory focus. The examples it uses to support its comments about the media are specific and indicate a range of knowledge beyond the obvious reference to Birmingham.

The March on Washington in 1963 demonstrated the importance of unity, popular support and the media as factors causing the Civil Rights Act to be passed. Nearly 250,000 people of all races, and representing the major civil rights organisations, walked to the Lincoln Memorial campaigning for 'jobs and freedom'. The march gained a lot of media attention and was a catalyst for change because it proved to Kennedy that he could not afford to ignore popular pressure for reform.

e The first sentence of this paragraph makes a new point and links to the previous three points. This integration suggests that the candidate is in the level 4 band. The final sentence links the March on Washington to the presidents — the focus of the next paragraph.

Presidential support for the act was another reason for its success. Martin Luther King's support of Kennedy in 1960 was an important factor in Kennedy's election. Therefore, King had some influence on the Kennedy administration, which he used to persuade Kennedy to back the bill. Kennedy's death in 1963 was also significant as it created much public sympathy for his civil rights agenda. Johnson, a supporter of the act, used the impetus created by Kennedy's death skilfully to persuade Congress to pass the bill. Presidential support was therefore essential to the passing of the Civil Rights Act — without it, Congress would never have accepted the bill.

The most significant factor that explains the passing of the Civil Rights Act was the March on Washington. It demonstrated the unity of the Civil Rights movement as King, members of the SNCC and CORE, and the leader of the NAACP, Roy Wilkins, threw their weight behind the protest. The march also gained considerable media attention, moving the public further behind the bill. Finally, the march forced the Kennedy administration to support the act publicly. In so doing, the march brought together important individuals such as King and Kennedy, without whom the success of the act would have been impossible.

e This conclusion shows again how the different factors described earlier in the response relate to each other. It draws conclusions about the relative importance of the different factors discussed and in this sense it is more than a simple summary.

e **This is a comprehensive, detailed and focused answer. It would achieve full marks by virtue of its thorough explanation of how the different factors interlink and its consideration of the relative importance of factors.**

Level 4: 40/40

Total: 58/60

■ ■ ■

C-grade answer

(a) The NAACP was founded in 1909 by a man called W. E. B. Dubois to campaign for the rights of African-Americans. It used the courts to show that segregation was wrong.

> 🖉 This introduction begins with two pieces of background information that are not made relevant to the question.

1944 was before the end of the Second World War but was still important. In 1944 there was a campaign called *Smith* v *Allwright*. This outlawed the white primary in Texas. The white primary was a system where you voted for a candidate who later stood in another election. Black people had not been allowed to vote in these elections. But after *Smith* v *Allwright* they could.

> 🖉 This paragraph is also irrelevant as it addresses a case that took place before the period specified in the question.

In 1946 there was a case called *Morgan* v *Virginia*. This was where it was decided that interstate travel could not be segregated any more. This was a big step forward as before this interstate travel had been segregated.

> 🖉 *Morgan* v *Virginia* is relevant to the question, but the description of the case here is brief and generalised. The candidate should have given more precise details.

In 1950, the Supreme Court passed judgement on *Sweatt* v *Painter*. This was a case to do with education and it said that black universities should be as good as white universities. The NAACP also changed education in 1954 with the Brown case. This was where a girl called Linda Brown had to walk a long way to go to a school for black people. Her father (Mr Brown) said that this was unfair and so schools were desegregated. Later, Brown II said that this should happen 'with all deliberate speed'.

The Montgomery Bus Boycott is outside this period but is also a time when the NAACP took steps to challenge Jim Crow laws.

> 🖉 Again, the candidate is discussing an event that is outside the period mentioned in the question.

In conclusion, the NAACP took lots of steps after the Second World War and achieved lots of desegregation for African-Americans.

> 🖉 This answer essentially gives a chronology of the NAACP's actions from 1944 to 1957 — the candidate misses the focus of the question because he/she makes no attempt to divide the answer into steps. The best part of the essay deals with education — it offers a series of details relevant to the question. However, parts of the essay fall outside the time period specified in the question and the discussion of *Morgan* v *Virginia* is poorly developed. This weak focus ensures that the essay would only achieve level 2.
>
> **Level 2: 10/20**

(b) In 1964 the much-needed Civil Rights Act was passed. The act was needed as black people were very unequal in the USA at the time. The act banned segregation in all public places and set up a department to make sure that black people had equal opportunities in their jobs. There is one main reason for the act, and that was President Lyndon B. Johnson who became president after Kennedy was shot. Kennedy was shot in 1963, stopping him from passing the Civil Rights Act.

> *e* The candidate states that there is only one reason for the passing of the Civil Rights Act. This is a simplistic view of events.

Although it was sad that Kennedy was shot, Johnson was able to pass the act because he said that it was what Kennedy would have wanted. This made people support it and made it easier to pass.

> *e* This paragraph gives a simplistic account of the significance of Kennedy's assassination.

Johnson also managed to get some Republicans to support the act. When the bill was passed, 152 Democrats and 138 Republicans supported it. Only 130 politicians were against it. This shows how important Johnson and cross-party support were as causes of the Civil Rights Act.

> *e* The candidate uses some specific supporting examples to good effect here.

Johnson was very persuasive and gave lots of speeches in favour of the act. He also got Truman, Eisenhower and Hoover (who had been presidents before Johnson) to support the act. His speeches were important as without them the act would not have been passed.

Johnson really cared for black Americans. He had a vision of a 'Great Society' in which African-Americans and whites would be equal. Johnson wanted his 'Great Society' to go further than Franklin Roosevelt's 'New Deal' and end poverty once and for all in the USA. He also wanted it to give equality of opportunity to all Americans, even African-Americans. This vision was an important factor in the passing of the act as it meant that Johnson was committed to the idea of black and white equality and so was prepared to fight for it even when people opposed him. This is different from Eisenhower's reaction when his Civil Rights Act was criticised — he backed down because he didn't really believe in it.

> *e* Although the expression is again simplistic, the candidate does make a relevant point, develops it with some accurate examples and explains how Johnson's ideology led to the passing of the act. This would place in the answer in the bottom bracket of level 3.

There were other factors that helped the passing of the Civil Rights Act, e.g. the civil rights campaigns in Little Rock, the March on Washington and Martin Luther King himself.

e The central weakness of this answer is its focus on Johnson. Although Johnson was important to the passing of the 1964 act, he was not the only cause. Other factors are mentioned in the conclusion, but they are entirely undeveloped. This answer would be awarded level 3 because of its developed and focused explanation of Johnson's ideology, its use of evidence of specific knowledge (e.g. the number of senators who voted for the act) and its sustained focus. However, this would be a low level 3 mark because of its weak explanatory links.

Borderline level 3: 23/40

Total: 33/60

Question 3

(a) How did the Civil Rights Act of 1964 help to realise the aspirations of African-Americans?

(20 marks)

(b) Why did the campaigns for black civil rights become increasingly militant in the late 1960s?

(40 marks)

Total: 60 marks

■ ■ ■

A-grade answer

(a) In 1964 President Johnson passed the Civil Rights Act, which was a significant step towards the realisation of the aspirations of many black Americans. The act was important in three main areas: it prohibited discrimination in public places, it established an Equal Employment Commission and it gave federal government the power to challenge 'Jim Crow' laws.

e The structure of the response is established in this introduction — this helps the examiner to understand the argument presented.

The ban on discrimination in public places was the first way in which the act addressed the aspirations of African-Americans. By October 1965, 214 cities had desegregated formally. The government also provided money to ensure that desegregation was possible in US schools. This led to a significant drop in the proportion of black children in segregated schools. The change realised the aspirations of black Americans as the NAACP had been challenging segregation since its foundation in 1909.

e This paragraph has a sustained focus on the aspirations of black Americans. It addresses the question in a clear and focused manner.

The act gave the Fair Employment Practices Commission the power to stamp out racial discrimination in the workplace. This aided the development of the black middle class. Between 1964 and 1968, black unemployment decreased by 34% and the percentage of African-Americans living below the poverty line decreased by a quarter. The powers of the commission were an important factor in meeting the aspirations of African-Americans because it made a significant step in addressing the causes of black poverty.

e The statistics here are impressive and a sign of secure development.

The act helped to realise the aspirations of African-Americans by giving the federal government the power to order desegregation formally. Thus, the act gave African-Americans a much greater chance of a fair hearing. The act also committed the federal government to acting swiftly to challenge segregation following successful

3

question

legal action. This met the aspirations of black Americans because it ensured that the courts and federal government had a duty to uphold the legal rights of black citizens.

In summary, the Civil Rights Act was an important step in meeting the black aspiration of racial equality. However, the act did not address other aspirations such as equal voting rights.

> 🖉 **This answer gets to grips with the question. The first two paragraphs after the introduction are well developed and have clear links to the question. The next paragraph is also linked clearly to the question, although it offers less detail. The conclusion is well written as it summarises the answer and goes on to suggest briefly that there were limits to the achievement of the act. Note that an answer that focused strongly on the limitations of the act would have risked failing to answer the question.**

Level 3: 19/20

(b) During the 1950s and early 1960s, the Civil Rights movement had achieved a number of key rulings. Throughout this time, campaigns focused on the southern states and on *de jure* change. However, in the mid-1960s a combination of frustration with slow progress and economic need led to violence becoming a characteristic of the Civil Rights movement.

> 🖉 This introduction is useful as it sets the question in its historical context and then addresses it directly.

Many black Americans were impatient with the rate of reform. Following the 1964 Civil Rights Act and the 1965 Voting Rights Act the pace of change slowed. This was for a number of reasons. First, the government's attention was no longer on civil rights issues; second, the prominence of black radicals was increasing; and third, Martin Luther King's influence was decreasing.

Progress in the years following 1965 seemed slow to many black Americans. The government felt that in overturning 'Jim Crow' with the Civil Rights Act and the Voting Rights Act (which abolished segregation and ensured political equality for black citizens) it had met the demands of black campaigners. Additionally, the Vietnam War distracted President Johnson, diverting both money and attention away from domestic issues. For these reasons, the tactics of non-violence seemed to be inadequate and militancy became increasingly attractive.

> 🖉 This final sentence is a good example of an explanatory link — this is needed in order to achieve a level 3 mark.

Following Malcolm X's Hajj, he changed his views significantly and accepted the idea that unity between himself and other civil rights campaigners was required. In his speech 'The Ballot or the Bullet' in the election year of 1964, Malcolm X recommended that black Americans should engage with the electoral process. As he dropped some of his more extreme views, his brand of Black Nationalism became increasingly attractive to African-Americans. The SNCC and the CORE's conversion to militancy in the late 1960s also caused a greater acceptance of radical methods and ideas in the black community.

At the same time, Martin Luther King and his methods were becoming less attractive. Many white people lost their sympathy for King when he spoke out against war in Vietnam. For African-Americans the failure of the Chicago Campaign of 1966 indicated that his methods and tactics were no longer effective. Additionally, King's Christian rhetoric was out of step with the culture of northern African-Americans, and in many ways King's southern middle-class upbringing meant that he did not understand the racial problems in the northern states. King's increasing marginalisation led to a movement away from his non-violent philosophy and therefore towards militancy.

Essentially it was the scale and nature of the problems facing African-Americans after 1965 that explain the turn to militancy. Social and economic problems such as northern ghettos, *de facto* discrimination in the workplace and widespread black poverty could not be solved simply by passing laws. Had it been possible to solve the problems of the northern states with legislation alone, it is arguable that Johnson would have taken steps to achieve this, that King's methods would have been more appropriate and that militant protest would seem disproportional.

Militancy was not a first choice for many black Americans, but by the late 1960s it had become a last resort.

e **This answer does almost everything it should. It discusses five factors in some detail and it is packed with explanatory links to the question. If the candidate had also attempted some integration, this answer would have been awarded a level 4 mark.**

Level 3: 34/40

Total: 53/60

■ ■ ■

C-grade answer

(a) Black Americans had many aspirations in 1964. For example, black Americans in the southern states wanted to see the end of segregation. Another aspiration that many black Americans had was to be treated fairly in their jobs. Black Americans also aspired to self-determination, especially in the late 1960s. The act met some of these aspirations but not all of them.

e This introduction shows some focus on the question and provides a context in which a good answer could be given. However, the candidate fails to make any reference to these aspirations in the rest of the essay.

question

The Civil Rights Act formally ended *de jure* segregation in the southern states. Following the Civil Rights Act, all public places, such as restaurants, theatres, libraries and transport, were desegregated legally. In effect, black people and white people had the same *de jure* rights in public places. Also, the Fair Employment Practices Commission was set up to guarantee equal opportunities for black citizens in the jobs market. Both of these parts of the act helped to realise the aspirations of black Americans.

> The final sentence of this paragraph attempts to link the point back to the question. However, the link is asserted rather than supported. The candidate should have linked these changes to the aspirations described in the introduction in order to produce a more sophisticated essay.

However, the Civil Rights Act did not do a lot of things. For instance, it did not bring about *de facto* self-determination for black people — there was nothing in the act to outlaw discrimination against black Americans when it came to voting. Also, the act did not produce an end to the ghettos in the northern cities. This is because *de facto* change is harder to achieve than *de jure* change. In both these ways, the Act did not help to realise the aspirations of black Americans.

> This paragraph addresses the limitations of the act in some detail, but it can not be credited because the question asks only for the ways in which the act *succeeded*.

In conclusion, in some ways the act did help meet the aspirations of black Americans, and in some ways it did not. For example, desegregation was achieved but self-determination was not.

> This answer contains only one developed statement relevant to the question. Therefore, the scope of the essay is limited, so it is awarded a mark at the lower end of level 2. Had the candidate linked the terms of the act to the discussion of aspirations in the introduction, the essay would have achieved a higher level 2 mark. The addition of specific supporting evidence could then have boosted this answer to level 3.

Level 2: 9/20

(b) In the early days of the Civil Rights movement it was not very militant at all. The black Civil Rights movement was much more militant after 1960 because of the Black Panthers and Malcolm X.

Malcolm X was a radical and militant Black Nationalist freedom fighter. In a famous picture he is seen holding a shotgun and looking out of a window. Malcolm X's father was able to build his own house and business. But the KKK burned his house down in 1929, and later murdered him when Malcolm X was six. Malcolm X taught that black people should fight back, 'an eye for an eye'. His father was a Baptist preacher, but Malcolm X was a Muslim and he did not believe in the Christian message of 'turning the other cheek'. Malcolm X was not in favour of desegregation like Martin Luther King, as he went to a mixed school that was run by whites. His English teacher told him to become a carpenter, not a lawyer, so he dropped out of school — he could see that white teachers did not encourage black children. When he moved to Harlem he was nicknamed 'Detroit Red' and he sold drugs and became a pimp. When he was caught he was sentenced to 10 years in prison. This was racist because he was a first-time offender and it made him militant. When in jail, he wanted to be free from prison but also from white people's power. He turned to the Nation of Islam and became a Muslim. The Nation of Islam said that white people were evil and would make black people slaves. This made Malcolm X militant against white people.

e This paragraph demonstrates considerable knowledge of Malcolm X's biography. However, most of the information is not targeted at the question.

Malcolm X had lots of followers. In 1964, he toured US universities giving a speech called 'The Ballot or the Bullet'. The speech persuaded many students to support his ideas. This increased the militancy of the movement because like him they believed that there could be no freedom under white people.

e The candidate makes a point here and then links it to the question with some relevant development.

The Black Panthers were militant as well as Malcolm X. They had a ten-point programme that was militant because it wanted all black people released from prison, even murderers and rapists, because the Panthers believed that all black prisoners were political prisoners. They also believed that the police were fascist and racist and that they could fight them if necessary. They organised a defence force to protect black people from racist attacks from white police and the KKK. The Black Panthers became very popular because one of their leaders was the victim of police racism. One of the first Black Panthers, Bobby Seale, protested about racism and was arrested for this protest. Huey Newton was another Black Panther who used militant methods. He was arrested for killing a white policeman. This made the Panthers more popular because the 'Free Huey' campaign struck a chord with northern African-Americans and gave a focus to the Panthers' activities.

e This paragraph is the reason that this essay reaches the level 3 mark band. It has a clear and relevant point, followed by adequate development, and concludes with a link back to the question.

The Black Panthers and Malcolm X had a big influence, and people became more militant. The film *Shaft* shows a group of Black Panthers fighting the mafia using militant methods. *Shaft* was very popular and made Black Power look exciting and glamorous, as did *Sweet Sweetback's Baadasssss Song,* which also turned the Panthers into heroes.

e *Shaft* and *Sweet Sweetback's Baadasssss Song* were released in 1971 — they are not relevant examples, as the question asks about the late 1960s.

question

Black militancy was more popular because of important figures and groups like the Black Panthers and Malcolm X, who had lots of followers who spread their militant ideas.

e This answer attempts to explain Malcolm X's militancy in terms of his personal history and is full of accurate details. However, many of these details do not address the question (e.g. Malcolm X's nickname 'Detroit Red'). Better selection would have helped this essay to focus more on the question. This response does have some good points — there are two instances that show explicit links to the question and some specific development. Consequently, this answer would achieve a borderline level 3 mark.

Borderline level 3: 23/40

Total: 32/60

Question 4

(a) What measures did the **US** federal government take to deal with racial inequality in the period 1945–57?   (20 marks)

(b) Why were Martin Luther King's campaigns in the southern states more successful than those in the northern states?   (40 marks)

Total: 60 marks

■ ■ ■

A-grade answer

(a) The US federal government took the following steps to deal with racial inequality between 1945 and 1957.

President Truman used his power as commander in chief of the armed forces to end segregation in the army, navy and air force in 1948. This meant an end to black-only mess halls, sleeping accommodation and transportation. It was a symbolic measure that indicated that the army recognised the contribution of black GIs during the Second World War. It also indicated a presidential interest in, and commitment to, the fight for racial equality.

This commitment was also evident in Truman's 1947 report *To Secure These Rights*. This report suggested a congressional act to end lynching, central government support for anti-segregation lawsuits and an end to segregation on interstate transport such as buses. Again, the report marked a symbolic commitment by the president to end racial discrimination and was part of Truman's campaign to demonstrate that the USA was the 'land of the free' during the Cold War.

Eisenhower, by contrast, had little commitment to the Civil Rights movement. Nonetheless, events in Little Rock, Arkansas in 1957 forced him to intervene. Following violence by white racists who were obstructing the African-American students attempting to enrol at Central High School, Little Rock, Eisenhower sent in the National Guard to restore order. In doing so, he threw the weight of federal government behind the Brown decision of 1954. This was significant as it showed the willingness of federal government to enforce the legal changes achieved by the NAACP.

The Civil Rights Act of 1957 could have been a significant step towards black emancipation, but it was sabotaged by southern Democrats and therefore its effectiveness was reduced significantly. The act proposed to guarantee voting rights to all citizens regardless of colour, and the establishment of a government department to deal with civil rights. However, Eisenhower was not committed sufficiently to the bill to defend it and consequently it added only 3% of black voters to the electoral rolls.

question

e This evaluation of the impact of Eisenhower's Civil Rights Act is sound. The candidate asserts that the act did little to help African-Americans and backs this up with a statistic.

By 1957, the federal government had taken steps to improve the status of African-Americans in the military, to uphold Supreme Court decisions regarding education, and to safeguard black voting rights. Essentially, however, all these steps were symbolic, because segregation remained a fact of life in education and it was not until the late 1960s that black voters truly enjoyed the same rights as white citizens.

e This conclusion attempts to link the previous paragraphs back to the question. However, the link is not proven but merely asserted. The answer concludes with some sound evaluation of the symbolic nature of many of the government's steps.

e **This answer considers four distinct factors, and each of the points made is supported with detailed examples. However, the candidate fails to make links to the question — the majority of links present are either unproven or implicit, and only the first paragraph attempts to explain the nature of the 'measures' taken. The answer is also long, so the candidate may not have left enough time to write an answer to part (b). This response would achieve a low level 3 mark, because there are some links to the question and there is sound evaluation in the last two paragraphs.**

Level 3: 18/20

(b) Martin Luther King was born in the south of the USA, so he understood its problems and its people. Through a series of successful campaigns he grew to be respected by southern African-Americans and to some extent became the spokesman of the Civil Rights movement in the southern states. However, by the time he turned his attention to the north of the USA, things had changed. The Civil Rights movement was no longer unified and he did not really understand what was going on in the northern states. Therefore, King was less successful in these states.

e This introduction is relevant to the question, but the discussion of the factors in the last sentence is simplistic.

King had more in common with the people he was fighting for in the southern states. King's Christian philosophy was more widely accepted by southern African-Americans who were predominantly Baptist, Methodist or Pentecostal. Therefore, when King organised non-violent demonstrations the protesters were willing to go along with this method, as they had a religious commitment to 'turning the other cheek'. In the urban north, formal religious commitment had been declining since the 1920s. As a result, King's message of 'agape love' meant nothing to African-Americans in this region. King was more successful in the southern states because his Christian message struck a chord there that it did not in the northern states, owing to the different social make-up of the two parts of the USA.

e This paragraph is a good example of how to structure an essay. It begins with a statement relevant to the question, continues with specific supporting evidence and ends with an explicit explanatory link.

Another reason for King's more limited success in the northern states was that he had less respect in this region. King was respected in the southern states because of his successful and high-profile campaigns in the area. By the time King arrived in the northern states he already had a reputation, but as northern African-Americans had not benefited from King's campaigns, they had less reason to respect and support him. King's campaigns never achieved decisive victories in the northern states, so his reputation never grew in this region. Without the respect of northern African-Americans, King was unlikely to be successful, because he would not enjoy popular support.

King's efforts in the northern states were also hampered by disunity in the Civil Rights movement. As King moved north, other organisations became more radical and embraced separatism, distancing themselves from the SCLC, which favoured racial integration. Southern campaigns had been successful because black people had been united, but without this unity King could not claim to be spokesman for the whole movement, so he had less chance of success in the northern region.

e Both this paragraph and the paragraph above make relevant points but fail to back them up with specific supporting examples. This weakens the overall answer.

Another factor contributing to King's failure in the northern states was that his tactics were no longer new and white authorities knew how to handle them. In the southern states, King was successful because of the mistakes of white authorities. 'Bull' Connor, for example, used police attack dogs and water cannons and arrested King. This provoked outrage and played into King's hands. Mayor Richard Daley on the other hand treated King with respect and agreed to negotiate with the SCLC. The lengthy negotiations which followed produced vague promises that did not improve anything for African-Americans. King was therefore less successful in the northern states because white people in this area had learned from the mistakes of 'Bull' Connor and were better at defusing King's campaigns.

e The candidate demonstrates understanding of the significance of Mayor Richard Daley to the question. However, the answer does not state explicitly that Daley was from a northern state — his relevance to the question is not made sufficiently clear.

The Chicago campaign taught King that the problems of the northern states were economic. He acknowledged that it was more difficult to solve economic problems than legal ones because this would require white people to give up their money (which they did not want to do). In the southern states however, desegregation did not require a large amount of spending. King was therefore less successful in the northern states because the problems in this region concerned money.

e This paragraph describes an important and relevant point, but it lacks detailed supporting evidence.

In conclusion, King was better equipped to deal with the problems in the southern states because he understood them, because they were not economic and because he had the respect of the African-Americans in this region. In the northern states this was not true, and King had the added difficulty of a disunited movement and white officials who had learned from the mistakes of 'Bull' Connor.

> This essay covers a range of different factors, puts forward some genuine explanation and has an unwavering focus on the question. Therefore, this answer would be awarded a level 3 mark for its range and explanatory focus. However, it would not achieve any higher than the middle of the mark band, because three of its points are supported in only a generalised fashion.

Level 3: 28/40

Total: 46/60

C-grade answer

(a) In 1945, Harry S. Truman became president of the USA. Before he became president he had publicly opposed lynching and racism. In 1946, Truman set up a committee to look into violence against African-Americans. In 1947 it made a report called *To Secure These Rights*. This report said that lynching should stop and that the government should support people campaigning for civil rights. In 1948 Truman desegregated the armed forces.

In private Truman was racist and he called African-Americans 'niggers'. This shows that he was not really committed to the civil rights of black people. But he did need black people to vote for him and in 1948 two-thirds of them did. Overall I think that Truman did care about African-Americans but mainly because he needed them to vote for him so that he could continue to be the president.

> This point about Truman's racism does not address the question and therefore cannot be credited.

However, Truman did not continue to be president because in 1952 Dwight D. Eisenhower took over. Although there were lots of campaigns while he was president he did not care about civil rights very much. He ignored the Montgomery Bus Boycott, even though it got lots of media attention. But he did send federal troops to protect the students at Little Rock so that they could go to school with white people. After he sent the troops the black children could go to that school even though no one wanted them there.

> The first half of this paragraph is irrelevant. The comment about Eisenhower sending in troops is relevant, but it is barely developed.

In 1957 Eisenhower passed the Civil Rights Act to try to ensure that black people could claim their right to vote. But it did not really change anything because he just did it to make people think that he liked African-Americans.

e This statement is developed in a limited manner.

In my opinion some things did happen during this period to make things better for African-Americans. For example, Eisenhower sent troops into Little Rock to protect the black students. However, overall nothing much really changed as Martin Luther King was not around at this time.

e This conclusion attempts to evaluate the progress made between 1945 and 1957. However, the evaluation is not supported and the reference to Martin Luther King is unnecessary.

e **This answer shows a combination of developed and undeveloped statements, and there is generally a strong focus on the question. The point about Truman's measures is securely developed and the discussion of Eisenhower's Civil Rights Act shows some development. However, the point regarding Little Rock is barely developed at all, and the paragraph about Truman's personal motives is irrelevant. This answer would achieve a mark in the middle of the level 2 band.**

Level 2: 12/20

(b) Many of Martin Luther King's campaigns in the southern states were successful. You only have to think about the Montgomery Bus Boycott and the Birmingham campaign to see this. In the northern states, particularly in Chicago, he was less successful. In this essay I am going to explain why Martin Luther King was so much less successful in the northern states than he was in the southern states by looking at a number of different factors.

e This introduction is clumsy. You should avoid writing about your own opinions, and there is no need to write 'In this essay I am going to…' because the examiner already knows this and it will only waste time.

There was a lot of disunity in the black movement after 1965. For example, the SNCC and the CORE were becoming more radical and even expelled white people from their organisations. This upset Martin Luther King who continued to support non-violence and said that you should always turn the other cheek. Also, Malcolm X, although dead, was growing in influence — further splitting the Civil Rights movement.

e The final sentence in this paragraph is unsupported and its link to the rest of the paragraph is unclear.

There was greater racism in the northern states. When Martin Luther King went there people threw bricks at him. He had not anticipated this as he had expected to achieve success. This made it hard for him to achieve his aims.

4

question

e This final sentence is an attempt at an explanatory link. However, it is weak — it does not explain why greater racism made the northern states more of a challenge for King.

Also, Martin Luther King was not known about in the northern region. People there just did not know who he was or why they should support him. In the southern states most people were Christians and so they supported him and his ideas about non-violence. In the northern states, people were not Christians and so they did not see why they should not fight back. As a result, King did not have much support in the northern states.

President Johnson was distracted by Vietnam at this time, so he was unable to help Martin Luther King. When Johnson and King had worked together they had been very effective. For example, Johnson had passed the Civil Rights Act of 1964 and the Voting Rights Act of 1965 after King's campaigns. King also criticised Vietnam, which upset Johnson.

In the northern states the problems were social and economic. Modern historians would point out that it is more difficult to change social and economic problems than political ones. For example, you can tell someone to give a black man a job, but it is hard to make the employer pay him the same as a white man. Not only were the problems social and economic, they had also been around for a long time.

The problems faced by Martin Luther King — northern racism, Vietnam and disunity in the Civil Rights movement — all meant that King was not as successful in the northern states as he had been in the south. All these factors are linked.

e This final sentence is an attempt to ensure that the answer achieves a level 4 mark. However, it cannot be credited as the statement is an unsupported assertion.

e **This response would achieve a level 2 mark — it considers a broad range of topics and generally develops these in a sound manner. It could not be awarded a level 3 mark, because it almost entirely lacks explanatory links to the question.**

Level 2: 20/40

Total: 32/60

Question 5

(a) What was the significance of the Montgomery Bus Boycott in the development of the civil rights campaign? (20 marks)

(b) Why were the leaders of the Civil Rights movement so often divided in the years 1964–68? (40 marks)

Total: 60 marks

■ ■ ■

A-grade answer

(a) Many historians have claimed that the Montgomery Bus Boycott marked a turning point in the campaign for civil rights. Although perhaps most famous for the way in which it brought Martin Luther King to the forefront, the boycott also proved the effectiveness of mass protest, especially when coupled with media interest.

The boycott is significant because it led to the emergence of Martin Luther King and the SCLC. Prior to this, there had been no clear leader of the black Civil Rights movement since W. E. B. Dubois in the early twentieth century. At the time of the boycott, King's role was that of spokesperson and figurehead. He organised the prayer meetings and fostered unity between black and white churches in Montgomery, thus increasing support for the boycott. Following the boycott, King became a figure of national importance, liaising with presidents and fronting a series of campaigns.

e This paragraph analyses effectively the significance of the boycott in two ways: it looks at events before the boycott to show how it brought about change, and it considers events following the boycott to show that this change was lasting.

The boycott is also significant because it was the first example of successful mass protest. Although the CORE had organised sit-ins before Montgomery, no protest on this scale had taken place. Following the success of the boycott, mass protest became a feature of many civil rights campaigns, including the March on Washington and the Greensboro sit-ins. In addition, the boycott showed that black people had economic power that white companies relied on. This was a significant shift away from the NAACP's campaigns, which focused on black people's constitutional rights and not their economic power as a group.

Finally, the boycott was significant because it demonstrated how the media could be manipulated to increase support for the civil rights campaigns. The nature of the boycott ensured that it attracted much media attention, and allowed people from all over the world to see the injustices of segregation. This increased the pressure on the government to bring about change. Many of the campaigns following the boycott used this strategy to their advantage, again demonstrating a shift in tactics.

In this way, the Montgomery Bus Boycott was significant because it changed the direction of the civil rights campaign and gave it a charismatic leader. Many historians have claimed that Montgomery was the beginning of the end for segregation.

ℓ **Every detail in this answer gets credited. Each paragraph is a relevant point, followed by a number of examples and a clear link to the question. The answer also considers the significance of the boycott by illustrating how it changed the civil rights campaign.**

Level 3: 20/20

(b) The divisions between the civil rights leaders were caused by the changing nature of the civil rights campaign and the failure of important initiatives in the late 1960s.

The shift in focus from southern segregation to northern poverty was a major reason for disunity in the late 1960s. The north presented different problems to the south. This led to disagreements over tactics. King decided to try non-violent direct action, which had been so successful in the southern states. However, when this failed in the Chicago Campaign he lost credibility. As a result, other groups with different methods grew in support. King, however, was committed deeply to non-violence and was unable to change. His refusal to change led to division because many African-Americans wanted a more radical solution which King would never support.

ℓ This paragraph makes a valid point but provides only generalised support. Nonetheless, there is an explanatory link to the question at the end of the paragraph.

Similarly, the successes and failures of campaigns involving African-Americans cooperating with white people created divisions between the different civil rights groups. The failure of the SNCC's Mississippi Freedom Summer in 1964 led to greater radicalism among SNCC activists. The Freedom Summer was designed to register black voters and to establish a legal black party to oppose the white-dominated Mississippi Democrats. Of the 800 students involved in the campaign, the majority were middle-class whites. When the campaign failed and the Democrats refused to back the proposed Mississippi Freedom Democratic Party, many black activists blamed the white campaigners. Soon after, the SNCC expelled all its white members. The SCLC, however, continued to have some success working with the Johnson administration to draft the Voting Rights Act.

ℓ The point made in this paragraph is supported excellently, but there is no explanatory link to the question.

The focus on economic and social problems that characterised the campaigns of the late 1960s also led to divisions. When the civil rights campaign had focused on the legal problem of segregation it was easy to agree on a solution — as the problem was legal, the resolution should also be legal. However, with economic and social problems there was a variety of possible approaches. King favoured reforms to the existing system, such as greater welfare provision. Malcolm X advocated a withdrawal from the system and black advancement through self-help. More radical still were the Black Panthers.

Influenced by the example of Marxist nationalism in less developed countries, they argued for a revolutionary attack on US capitalism.

e This paragraph shows excellent development, but there is no explanatory link to the question.

Radical groups also criticised older civil rights leaders. Many of them thought that King was too involved with the US government. The Black Panthers argued that King was a tool of white power and that essentially his role was to keep black people in their place. These criticisms split the Civil Rights movement into those such as the NAACP and the SCLC, who would work with white people, and the CORE, the SNCC and the Black Panthers, who would not work with white people because they saw this as selling out African-Americans.

e This paragraph develops points well and makes explanatory links to the question.

Personal rivalries also explain the criticisms of King and the SNCC's desire to develop its own identity. In the early 1960s, the SNCC was often seen as the student wing of the SCLC. Huey Newton and Stokely Carmichael of the SNCC were not happy with this and wanted an independent profile. Consequently, personal factors caused divisions in the Civil Rights movement because Newton and Carmichael were not happy to be eclipsed by King.

There is no single reason why the leaders of the Civil Rights movement were so often divided in the 1960s, but perhaps the most important factor was the changing nature of the problems they were trying to tackle.

e In this conclusion, the candidate attempts to integrate the answer by discussing the relative importance of factors. However, as there is no justification given for the conclusion reached by the candidate, this answer would not achieve higher than a level 3 mark.

e **This answer is written in a sophisticated style and has many virtues. However, it is not consistent in either its use of supporting evidence or its explanatory links. It would therefore not be awarded more than a solid level 3 mark.**

Level 3: 30/40

Total: 50/60

■ ■ ■

C-grade answer

(a) In 1955 a lady called Rosa Parks refused to give up her seat to a white man on a bus in Montgomery. This sparked the Montgomery Bus Boycott when for almost 1 year African-Americans boycotted the buses in the city. They refused to travel by bus and instead walked or sometimes shared lifts in their cars.

question

📝 This introduction contains accurate information about the boycott but makes no attempt to focus on the question. An introduction should demonstrate an appreciation of the demands of the question.

When Rosa Parks refused to give up her seat to a white man because she was tired, she could not have known what her actions would lead to. When the bus companies discovered that lots of their money came from black customers and that now that there were no black customers they were losing money, they were not happy. They wanted the black customers back.

📝 The candidate displays some knowledge, but shows no explicit focus on the question. The reference to the bus company could be credited as an implicit attempt to answer the question.

Martin Luther King did not want to be involved in the boycott but was made to be. King and his organisation, the Southern Christian Leadership Conference (SCLC), coordinated the people who did not ride on the buses. King also gave some inspiring speeches. Later in 1963 he gave an inspiring speech called 'I Have a Dream'. His speeches brought black people together. Before the Montgomery Bus Boycott nobody had heard of Martin Luther King, but afterwards he was really famous and involved in lots of other campaigns.

📝 Although this paragraph contains some irrelevant information (such as the reference to King's 1963 speech) it is the first time the candidate tackles the question head on. The final sentence is weak, but it is focused on the question.

At the end of the Montgomery Bus Boycott the government decided that it needed black people to go back on the buses, so it said that black people and white people should be able to sit in the same seats. This was called desegregation and is what the black people had wanted. It meant that they were now equal to white people. This was significant because it was the first time that lots of black people had worked together to achieve a change in the law.

📝 The candidate can be credited for focusing on the question and especially for considering significance. However, the information in this paragraph is generalised and in places inaccurate.

The Montgomery Bus Boycott was significant because it introduced the world to Martin Luther King and it got African-Americans what they wanted. It was the first time that this had happened.

📝 **This response demonstrates that the candidate has some understanding of the significance of the Montgomery Bus Boycott. There are two occasions where the candidate makes an attempt to focus on the question and there is some explicit reference to the significance of the events. However, the supporting evidence is either weak or unfocused and as a result the answer would achieve a level 2 mark.**

Level 2: 11/20

(b) The Civil Rights movement was made up of a number of different groups with different goals. Groups such as the CORE, the SNCC and the NAACP, as well as Martin Luther King's SCLC, helped to organise black people in opposition to white racism. However, in the late 1960s the movement became increasingly divided.

ℓ This introduction defines the Civil Rights movement as being made up of several organisations. This sets the context for the rest of the answer.

Martin Luther King had run a number of campaigns successfully since the Montgomery Bus Boycott with a mixture of policies designed to end segregation. However, he refused to back down over his principle of non-violence, which was designed to win media support for the black struggle. Other groups, such as the SNCC and the Black Panthers, were prepared to use force where necessary — for example, in the Watts Riots of 1966.

ℓ This paragraph is focused on the question and is developed well, but it lacks any explanation.

In the Montgomery Bus Boycott, King had shown himself to be a strategic genius. Without a doubt King was the reason why the SCLC won the battle in Montgomery. However, King's tactics in Chicago failed to achieve any significant success and therefore he lost support. As a result, other civil rights groups gained support as they offered a more radical alternative.

ℓ This paragraph concludes with an explanatory link — this takes the answer into the level 3 mark band because of the strong focus and secure development of the preceding paragraphs.

Another reason why the Civil Rights movement split was because it started to focus on social and economic issues. In the southern states the movement had focused on *de jure* change (a change in the law). However, in the northern states, the movement was fighting for *de facto* change (a change in reality). This was much harder to achieve and meant that people were divided over how to achieve it.

Probably the most important reason why the leaders of the Civil Rights movement were so often divided in the years 1964–68 was that there was a lot of personal bad feeling between them. Martin Luther King was meant to be a saint, but he had lots of affairs which his wife knew about. Some people said that he wasn't a saint, but a sinner — this caused divisions. Before his death, Malcolm X did not like Martin Luther King and called him an 'Uncle Tom' because he worked with white people. The fact that King and Malcolm X did not like each other is another factor explaining why the movement was divided.

ℓ The final point is simplistic but it offers a further explanatory link to the question.

There were other factors that created divisions within the Civil Rights movement. For example, King disagreed with President Johnson over the Vietnam War. King thought that the war was wrong, but Johnson was commander in chief of the army fighting the war. This division meant that Johnson was less likely to support King.

e This paragraph is relevant, but the candidate has not drawn out the implications of his/her comments to show how Johnson and King's disagreement led to divisions in the movement.

It can therefore be seen that divisions were caused by personal rivalries and the Vietnam War, as well as social and economic problems in the northern states. However, criticisms of Martin Luther King were put to one side after his death in 1968.

e **The essay is focused on the question and it has some range. This answer would achieve a level 3 mark because of its two explanatory links. It would merit only a low mark within this band, however, because there are few links and the development is simplistic in places.**

Level 3: 23/40

Total: 34/60